Readings in
Early Childhood
Music Education

Readings in Early Childhood Music Education

COMPILED AND EDITED BY
BARBARA L. ANDRESS AND LINDA MILLER WALKER

 MUSIC EDUCATORS NATIONAL CONFERENCE

Contents

Section 3   A New Look

Introduction

Two areas of deep concern for American society are becoming increasingly intertwined: our failure to educate the ever-increasing numbers of disadvantaged children and the growing demand for child care for families across the socioeconomic spectrum. [1]

 his statement, an outgrowth of a three-year Bank Street study of early childhood programs, brings to our attention the ever-growing involvement of the public schools in early childhood education.

Many music educators have viewed early childhood music education with peripheral interest, always sympathetic to the need for quality experiences, interested in assisting, but only to a point. We have not seriously envisioned such programs as a part of the public school system—programs that might indeed become teaching responsibilities for us. More and more, preschool children are being included in the public schools, and with that trend comes the need for quality music education programs that are either serviced directly by the music teacher, shaped by inservice training, or otherwise influenced by experts in music education.

We are beginning to see agencies, such as state departments of education and social services departments, working together to solve problems and fund educational components that involve training programs and delivery systems for various child-care systems. Innovative programs with parenting components thrust the influence of the educator even more directly into the home and the early life of the child. We suddenly need to provide information on appropriate developmental practices and programs in music education to meet the unique needs of the preschool special learner.

As a profession, we have not been idle in our studies of how young children interact with music. We must, however, remain on the cutting edge of this rapidly developing social trend. We must view our perimeters beyond the traditional public-school levels to include the various early childhood administrative agencies.

In the first section of this book we consider the development of the young child. In the second section we take a second look at articles previously published in our profession's journals. The purpose of reprinting these articles is to provide ready access for those who may have missed these materials and, in some cases, to instill a sense of the historical evolution of early childhood music education. The materials also provide an informational review and foundation for those newly entering the field of early childhood music.

Topics covered include the early childhood educator's view of how young children learn; child growth and development and implications for developmentally appropriate musical behaviors; topical information on song acquisition, vocal ranges, and song mastery; spontaneous musical play; design of music learning environments; and the value of movement and music experiences in the young child's learning.

New articles included in this book focus on topics that currently concern early childhood music educators, such as young children's ability to utilize critical thinking in their musical play; the look of a developmentally appropriate, early childhood, multicultural music program; musical experiences of prekindergarten children at risk; and guidelines for assessing young children's musical behaviors.

Now, more than ever, the public demands a quality learning component in the childcare setting. No longer is society satisfied with simple custodial care for young children. The time to understand, refine, and promote our approaches to early childhood music education is now. We may not receive a second invitation to contribute to the various programs being planned: We must see to it that our initial contacts bear fruit for those who must deal with the education of young children today.

—*Barbara L. Andress*
and Linda Miller Walker

Note

1. *Executive Summary, Early Childhood Programs and the Public Schools: Between Promise and Practice* (New York, NY: Bank Street College, 1988).

A Look at
the Child

The early childhood community encourages an individually and developmentally appropriate program for young learners. Efforts to plan effective musical experiences for young children must begin with a comprehensive understanding of the child's total growth and development. In this article, Stevie Hoffman summarizes information on children's physical, social-emotional, and cognitive growth, and also includes references for a more comprehensive study of each developmental area. Such information provides a theoretical base for planners who adopt a constructivist position and for those who take other philosophical stances as they consider how children learn in the early childhood years.

Growing and Learning in the Early Childhood Years

BY STEVIE HOFFMAN

oet Margaret Wise Brown tells children that the important thing is "that you are you."[1] Helping children discover that important thing in each of them grows out of what we know about the similarities in young children's growth and development and the extent to which we understand and value the differences that make each child special and unique. Teachers of young children must determine developmentally appropriate curriculum practices from a working knowledge of current understandings about child development and learning. In other words, what teachers believe about children as learners is reflected in the decisions those teachers make to enable the learning process.

The purpose of this chapter, therefore, is three-fold. First, it serves as a brief reminder of what we know about the child under the age of six—while highlighting similar developmental patterns of all young children. Second, it considers how children learn in the early childhood years. Third, the chapter offers suggestions about how knowledge of prekindergarten children can aid teachers in designing appropriate curricula.

The Developing Child

Within the wide variances of what is viewed as normal physical, socioemotional, and cognitive development, we are aware of a predictable continuum or pattern of growth during children's young lives. Children are very much alike in that they do grow and their development is ongoing. We also know that both genetic and environmental factors contribute to this growth and development. These factors result in the differences that we recognize in children of the same chronological age.

Physical development: We expect to see children differ in size and physical ability. They may be tall or short, slender or not. Some are able to jump and hop on one foot. Some jump, hop, and skip with agility. The motor development of children of the same age is as varied as their height and weight.

We can predict, however, that physical and motoric characteristics of young children follow a developmental continuum. For example, as the infancy period disappears and children become walkers, runners, and jumpers rather than creepers and crawlers, they are appropriately described as toddlers: "uncertain about their bodies...with a look of toddling, of not being really sure of their control over large muscles."[2]

We also know that body proportions change dramatically during the early growing years, and that much of the weight gained during this time can be attributed to muscular development. Given time for this skeletal and muscular growth and given activities that encourage them to try out what their growing and developing bodies can do, children begin to gain increased control over their physical movements. In other words, they crawl, walk, run, jump, hop, and skip when their bodies are mature enough and when they are able to control the large muscles used in these gross motor skills.

The small muscles, however, develop at a slower rate. The coordination required for more complex motor movements—catching a small ball, using a hula hoop, walking on a narrow balance beam, or even striking a single tone bar on a xylophone—takes growing time and lots of activity time for developing voluntary control of all of the fine muscle movements.

From birth through the preschool years, children advance greatly in their physical strength and coordination. When they are encouraged to move in ways appropriate to their particular stage of physical growth, their agility and coordinated motor skills develop naturally over time. As they become increasingly sure of their physical abilities, their confidence helps them reach out and explore new tasks with greater certainty.

Social and emotional development: Social and emotional developmental processes also progress through predictable stages. Although emotional growth appears to be influenced the most by significant others in children's everyday learning environment, their early social behaviors are closely aligned with Piaget's concept of egocentric thought.

Piaget used the term *egocentricism* to label the normal cognitive stage of children's thinking in which they are unable to understand that someone else has a different point of view than their own.[3] Identification of this stage provides an explanation for why young children often have difficulty sharing and cooperating with one another. Not until children are able to cognitively internalize the fact that other children may have different needs and ideas, and not until they can consider these needs and ideas in their interactions with others, can children enter into more positive social relationships. At that point, we see the development of collaborative efforts as well as friendships that are more lasting. These are important steps in children's awareness and acceptance of others as equally unique individuals.

Erickson proposed that all humans develop emotionally within predictable "either/or" patterns.[4] Three of his eight psychosocial stages—basic trust, autonomy, and initiative—have particular relevance to children's emotional growth during the first five or six years of their lives.

In the year of infancy, basic trust is established—a positive feeling toward others and one's self—or mistrust that results in feelings of insecurity or fear. Basic trust enables children to feel good about themselves and leads to increasing willingness and confidence in relating to others. Mistrust, on the other hand, grows out of unmet needs or unpredictable adult behaviors and manifests itself in behaviors that indicate a lack of self-esteem and an inability to deal with the immediate world.

During the next year or so, and guided by understanding adults, children grow in their sense of self-control and independence. They begin to move toward what Erikson called autonomy—the ability to make one's own decisions about what, when, how, and why to feel, think, and act. This very positive emotional development leads to pride in one's personal self and actions. However, when children are subjected to constant rejection of ideas, ridicule, or pressure to conform to inappropriate expectations, they experience such a sense of failure that autonomy becomes impossible. Erikson labeled this result as one of shame with regard to their feelings and doubt about their abilities.

The third psychosocial-emotional stage of child development early childhood teachers must consider is initiative, which occurs within the two or three years prior to kindergarten entrance when children build upon their successes as infants and toddlers. They have learned much, seem to have unlimited energy, and derive pleasure from just doing things. At the same time, they are also eager to learn and will stay with an activity they choose, working toward goals they set for themselves with the support of adults they trust.

If children have only limited experiences to develop this sense of what they can and should do, they may act in ways that result in feelings of guilt or incompetence. They constantly wrestle with their own physical and emotional responses as well as the limitations put on their behavior by others. They are not always able or permitted to do what they want without consequences. When children are able to respond positively to these conditions of emotional development, they demonstrate Erikson's notions of the stage of initiative. But when they have not been able to come to terms with these conditions, Erikson maintains that guilt could become a serious threat to their emotional growth.

Like physical development, social and emotional growth is predictable in an "either/or" continuum. However, the conditions for their development rests far more within children's learning environment—especially, the human environment—than in genetic makeup.

Cognitive development: Cognitive development also progresses along a continuum with each stage building from and on the previous one. Piaget addressed this development of knowledge in terms of operations: "a set of actions modifying the object, and enabling the Knower to get at the structures of the transformation."[5] Piaget explained an operation as an internalized action, never isolated but always linked to other operations. Furthermore, he maintained that during the period of preoperational representations—sometime between two and eight years of age—children's thinking was not operational as he had defined that term.

In this same writing, Piaget also addressed four factors related to cognitive growth, none of which he believed could stand alone to suffi-

ciently explain children's development from one set of cognitive structures (or schema) to another.[6] Maturation is one of these factors that must be considered. However, the chronological age when each cognitive stage appears varies so much among children within and between cultures that maturation in and of itself does not provide an adequate explanation for cognitive development.

Experience is also a related factor, but, for Piaget, not sufficient to explain cognitive growth. This can be understood when we consider his definitions of experience. He discussed physical experience and defined this as taking action upon objects and formulating some knowledge about those objects: for example, holding two objects and noting that one is heavy and one is light. On the other hand, he defined logical-mathematical experience from the point of view of knowledge coming from "actions of the subjects" (what the child does to the object) and not just an experience with the objects themselves. Seeing or even holding a tambourine and a tom-tom provides a physical experience for a child. But, the child's own actions—actually shaking the tambourine and beating on the drum—can provide an experience for cognitive connection-making, a logical-mathematical experience in Piagetian terms, and makes possible "knowingness" for the child.

Social transmission (imparting information through language or teaching per se) is a third factor that Piaget believed was insufficient to explain cognitive development. The development of knowledge is possible only if the child has the psychological structure to enable the assimilation, organization, and adaptation of the information.

The fourth factor related to cognitive growth is equilibration, the term Piaget used for what he called the active process of self-regulation or compensation. When there is a discrepancy between what children have come to think and new information, assimilation and accommodation are not in balance and the restructuring of knowledge is limited. This adaptation process begins when children react in ways that compensate for the mismatch. They often make reasonable learning "errors" in that they attempt unworkable actions upon objects or assign unconventional reasons for events. These actions and reasons indicate varying levels of compensation for discrepancies. However, Piaget maintained that equilibration is not achieved until learners understand how and why their actions modify or in some way change the object, event, or concept with which they are interacting.

The onset of the preoperational period begins when children are able to substitute a mental image or word for something that is not actually present. This representation makes it possible for thought to be faster and less rooted in immediate action. Children can think about more than one thing at a time; they can remember events in the past and can contemplate what they will do another time. Most importantly, children are able to translate their thoughts and feelings through language and symbolic representation that communicate more effectively and efficiently to others.

However, Piaget noted four limitations in children's cognitive processing during the preoperational stage of development. One is a difficulty in being able to focus on more than one aspect of a situation or property at the same time and understand the relation between these. A second limitation is that children may be able to focus on the beginning and ending of a process but not conceptualize the in-between steps in the process. Third, it is difficult for children to reconsider what they have already concluded. The last limitation, according to Piaget, is a hallmark of egocentric thought—expecting that others view things and events in the same way. Once more, we must remember that chronological age is not the determinant of progress through developmental stages; the developmental sequence of cognition, however, is invariant.

The Learning Child

Highlighting the characteristics of preoperational thought provides a theoretical base from a constructivist position for considering how chil-

dren learn in the early childhood years. First, they must be actively engaged in the learning process. Children must actively explore the materials and events in their learning environment to discover how their own actions can effect change. These operations make possible children's formulation of notions, tentative as these may be at any given time, and are at the core of knowledge.

In child-initiated, child-directed explorations and discovery processes, children construct personally meaningful ways for making things work. This indicates the importance of children being able to self-select the materials with which they wish to work and being able to work with them in their own ways. When this self-selection is encouraged, children take control of their own learning and learning is enhanced.

Children revise their understandings as they work with familiar materials. This does not mean that they have the same experiences with the same materials or events, but that they use familiar materials under different conditions and in different settings. This provides opportunities for them to make new connections or to revise conclusions about what they might or can do.

Children learn when new information or experience is closely related to what is familiar or known. Potential discrepancies between the known and the unknown are important to the learning process; however, materials and experiences must not be so novel as to be rejected by the children.

Children learn from one another as well as from the adults in their environment. Sometimes the experiences of children lead them to draw independent conclusions. As a result, the child demonstrates potential to revise or reconsider existing schema. Children learn best when adults in the learning environment are responsive to their perceived need-to-know and are supportive and accepting of their efforts to know. Because knowledge is not a copy of reality, learning occurs only when children are able to make personal connections—not when children are pushed to meet adult expectations and to reproduce the adult's perceptions of an end product or conclusion. The result of such conforming to reality reduces the cognitive risk-taking so necessary in learning. Children, therefore, become most successful in their learning when errors in decisions are not considered wrong but are treated as part of the construction and reconstruction of knowledge. This suggests that children learn best when the processes and the tentative understandings involved in learning are valued as much as if not more than the products. Children learn best when they feel good about themselves as learners and know that their learning efforts will be supported. As they become more competent they gain confidence in their abilities and efforts and are eager to consider that which they have not yet explored and discovered.

Language, an Observable Key to Learning

The interrelatedness of language and thought and its implications for the child's growing understanding was expressed years ago by Earl Kelley in his book, *Education for What Is Real.*[7] He wrote that things around us have no meaning except the meaning we ascribe to them; that they are nothing until we make them something; and then they are only what we mean them to be. If we listen thoughtfully to what children say, we can learn much about what they have learned and how they are learning.

Halliday referred to children's use of language to represent their ideas and feelings as "learning to mean"—learning through and with language.[8] In other writings, Halliday reflected on language as "sociosemiotic" in which meanings are constructed by children as they interact with significant others who are more proficient language users.[9] In this exchange of meanings, children try to make sense out of their world of people, places, things, and happenings. Smith's elaboration of the process states:

> [This] theory of what the world is like...is the basis of all our perception and understanding of the world; it is the root of all learning, the source of all hopes and fears, motives and expectancies, reasoning and creativity.... If we can learn at all, it is by modifying and elaborating our theory.[10]

The positions of these two scholars, along with other contemporary theory-into-practice researchers and writers, support a view that the growth of language is a continuous process, is rooted in cognitive growth, involves children as active participants in the learning process rather than passive bystanders, and is aided by an environment that is geared toward children's ways of learning, responsive to the child, focused on meaning first rather than form and product, and that rejoices in children's intent and expression of that intent. This view of language learning and use is closely aligned with Piaget's theory of children constructing knowledge within the context of both cognitive and social transactions.[11]

If language and learning are interrelated, then language must enhance thought just as cognitive growth enhances language. In her text, *Children's Language and Learning*, Lindfors discusses how children's own use of language as well as the language of other children and adults enables cognitive processing. Her discussion focuses on language enabling:

> . . . retrieval of past experiences and understanding of those experiences, ideas and feelings; . . . reinterpretation of these data in new or different light; . . . going beyond the present to speculate and hypothesize what might be, or going beyond what is real into the world of imagination; . . . going beyond personal experiences to empathize with others and to see their points of view; . . . making meanings more precise so that others understand what is being shared; . . . seeking

information, clarifying ideas, questioning that which is uncertain; and...focusing attention on what one is doing to aid in comprehending and, therefore, learning. [12]

When language is viewed from this perspective, we can hear the cognitive connections children make as they wrestle with constructing their personal view of the world about them. However, language can enhance thought only when children are actively engaged in this transactive process. This means that children must be in learning environments where children's talk is invited, responded to, and valued as a most significant aspect of all learning. Only then do children become what Wells labels in the title of his book, *The Meaning Makers: Children Learning Language and Using Language to Learn*. [13]

Making Connections for Teachers

What does all of this mean for teachers of young children? It means that the language of teaching becomes the enabler of the language of learning, a position supported by the research of many others. [14]

If using language makes cognitive processing possible for children, then adults must not only invite children into dialogues where they can express their own personal understandings, we must also respond to what children intend to mean in ways that enhance their thought connections. If when asking children questions, for example, adults expect a particular "correct" answer, that expected response is all that will be given. If adults only direct what is to be said or provide all of the information to be considered by the young learner, then children only repeat the adult or have limited, if any, information to add.

On the other hand, if the questions of adults are sincere—seeking information that is not al-ready known by the adult and perceived by children as inviting expressions of their own "knowingness"—then, a meaningful dialogue with "real language" is possible. Children can respond using language to share ideas and feelings gained from previous experiences, they can elaborate on what and how and why they "mean," they can revise existing interpretations based on new evidence, and they can hypothesize what might be. Invitations into dialogues, both with adults and with other young learners, encourage children to take more control of their learning, seeking new information and clarification of that with which they are unsure.

The response of adults to children plays an even more significant role in the language of learning. Support for children's connection-making, confirmation of their initial interpretations, provision of appropriate cues for potential reconsiderations are all heard by children in the language responses of adults. The language of teaching, in these instances, leads to cognitive risk-taking for young learners. However, when children are limited or not supported in their personal language of learning, learning can be thwarted or ended for many youngsters.

In an interview addressing "Talk and Learning in the Classroom," Anthony Adams warned that children "switch off" when they are "prohibited in the use of self-expressive talk." [15] He also stated that classrooms should be places where teachers "learn from their students...are manipulators of the sources from which pupils are able to learn [and are] collaborators in learning with pupils, exploring problems together." [16] These interview comments suggest that learning experiences and materials must entice learning and that understanding and appreciating the role of talk in children's learning may necessitate changes in how teachers view both teaching and learning.

Teachers have a responsibility to enable children's learning. That's what teaching is all about: helping children move toward desired intellectual and social-moral autonomy by valuing their ways of learning, trusting their construction and reconstruction of knowledge and responding to what children mean as they use language. Implementing developmentally appropriate curriculum practices for young learners demands nothing less from those who enable the learning of all children.

Creating a learning environment in which the physical surroundings provide opportunities for child-initiated activities with familiar and unfamiliar materials and for teacher-initiated experiences to extend children's learning sets the stage for an appropriate curriculum. Moreover, creating a learning environment where the human component of the environment accepts and values the unique characteristics of each child and invites all children into the learning experiences ensures instructional strategies that match their varied ways of learning during these early childhood years.

In whatever capacity teachers work with young children in educational settings, children's own personally meaningful construction of knowledge must be enabled. Teaching from a constructivist's position make this possible. But, what a positive influence teaching from this perspective can have on the developing learner—for it says to the child that the important thing is "that you are you."

Notes

1. M. W. Brown, *The Important Book*, First Harper Trophy ed. (New York: Harper & Row, 1990).
2. C. Seefeldt, *Teaching Young Children* (Englewood Cliffs, NJ: Prentice Hall, 1980), 40.
3. J. Piaget, "Development and Learning," in *Piaget Rediscovered: A Report on the Conference on Cognitive Studies and Curriculum Development*, ed. R. Ripple and V. Rockcastle (1964): 223–37.
4. E. Erickson, *Identity: Youth and Crisis* (New York: W. W. Norton & Co., 1968).
5. Ripple and Rockcastle, *Piaget Rediscovered*, 228.
6. J. Piaget, in *Piaget Rediscovered*, 230–34.
7. E. Kelley, *Education for What Is Real* (New York: Harper, 1947).
8. A. K. Halliday, *Learning How to Mean: Explorations in the Development of Language* (New York: Elseview North Holland, 1975).
9. A. K. Halliday, *Language as Social Semiotic: The Social Interpretation of Language and Meaning* (Baltimore: University Park Press, 1978).
10. F. Smith, *Reading Without Nonsense* (New York: Teachers College Press, 1979), 79.
11. See for example, *How Children Construct Literacy: Piagetian Perspectives* ed. Y. Goodman (Newark: International Reading Association, 1990).
12. J. Lindfors, *Children's Language and Learning* (New York: Prentice Hall, 1987), 263–73.
13. G. Wells, *The Meaning Makers: Children Learning Language and Using Language to Learn* (Portsmouth, NH: Heinemann Educational Books, 1986).
14. S. Hoffman, "The Language of Teaching: Responses to Children's Developing Literacy," *Childhood Education* 63 (1987): 356–62; S. Hoffman with L. Lilja, "The Teacher's Role in Fostering Young Children's Language Learning Through Storybook Reading," *Yearbook* (National Reading and Language Arts Educators, 1989), 71–96; J. Janes and S. Hoffman, "The Effects of In-Service Education on the Teachers' Role in Encouraging Children's Language Learning Through Storybook Reading," *Yearbook* (National Reading and Language Arts Educators, 1990), 179–94. See also K. Berry, "Talking to Learn Subject Matter: Learning Subject Matter Talk," *Language Arts* 62 (1985): 34–43; and D. Dillon and D. Searle, "The Role of Language in One First-Grade Classroom," *Research in the Teaching of English* 15 (1981): 311–28.
15. D. Searle, "Talk and Learning in the Classroom: An Interview with Anthony Adams," *Language Arts* 61 (1984): 120.
16. Searle, "Talk and Learning," 123.

Stevie Hoffman is professor of education at the University of Missouri—Columbia.

SECTION 2

A Second Look

Ideas That Have Impacted on
Today's Early Childhood Music Education

Music educators can review early issues of *Music Educators Journal* and other MENC publications and note with interest and pride that they contained writings on the topic of music for preschool children. These materials demonstrate MENC's long-term commitment to quality education for this age-group.

Early contributors reported on the application of approaches such as Montessori, the Pillsbury Foundation, and Dalcroze, or reflected on their own special research findings, beliefs, and methods. Some of these materials have been selected for a second look. Their usefulness may be viewed from a historical perspective or as a mark of their continued credibility and value in today's program planning. The compilers of this document also reached out for pertinent articles published in other professional journals that may not have been readily available to the music educator. Together, these articles will help music educators explore the following topics:

Learning From Others in the Field of Early Childhood Education. The importance of networking with other organizations, learning their perspective of developmental profiles of young children, and sharing their rationale for how one interacts with this age-group is highlighted by the inclusion of "Guidelines for Developmentally Appropriate Practice in Early Childhood Programs Serving Children from Birth Through Age Eight" as excerpted from a publication of the

National Association for the Education of Young Children.

What Happens in Early Childhood Music. John Feierabend's article describes music in early childhood providing one answer to what happens in early childhood music.

On How Musical Sounds Begin. Two articles explore how musical sounds begin: Howard Gardner's "Do Babies Sing a Universal Song?" and Donald Pond's article on "The Young Child's Playful World of Sound."

The Merit of Early Beginnings. This topic is addressed in two articles: "No Age Is Too Early to Begin" by Frances Webber Aronoff and "Awakening the Artist: Music for Young Children" by Dorothy McDonald and Jonny Ramsey.

An Environment in Which Music Can Happen. Concerns for the learning environment are dealt with in a revised chapter from the 1974 MENC book *Music in Early Childhood*.

As with any compilation of writings on a given topic, the compilers found many articles truly worthy of reprinting. Space restraints always limit what can be included, and choices are difficult. The compilers hope that these few representational readings will entice you to search out and gather your own complete collection of worthy early childhood music education resources.

Upon entering the field of early childhood education, the music educator finds that much research has been accomplished and many valid curricula implemented by those who have worked for many years to understand how the young child grows and learns. Many national, state, and local professional organizations provide leadership and materials for caregivers and teachers of this age-group, including the National Association for the Education of Young Children (NAEYC) and the Association for Childhood Education International (ACEI). Music educators can learn from such experts and contribute to the existing bank of knowledge: It is not necessary to reinvent the wheel but rather more expeditious to profit from the experience of others in the field. Moving within the early childhood community's curricular expectations is a viable route to effecting positive changes for the music education of this age-group. The following excerpts from the NAEYC Position Statement provide important information as to the philosophical and curricular stance of the nation's early childhood educators. Music educators will have little problem in accepting these stated positions because the comments reflect quality and developmental concerns that have been a part of our program projections for many years.

Developmentally Appropriate Practice in Early Childhood Programs Serving Children from Birth Through Age Eight

❖

NATIONAL ASSOCIATION FOR THE EDUCATION OF YOUNG CHILDREN

he National Association for the Education of Young Children (NAEYC) believes that a high-quality early childhood program provides a safe and nurturing environment that promotes the physical, social, emotional, and cognitive development of young children while responding to the needs of families. Although the quality of an early childhood program may be affected by many factors, a major determinant of program quality is the extent to which knowledge of child development is applied in program practices—the degree to which the program is *developmentally appropriate*. NAEYC believes that high-quality programs should be available to all children and their families.

In this position paper, the concept of developmental appropriateness will first be defined. Then guidelines will be presented describing how developmental appropriateness can be applied to four components of early childhood programs; curriculum, adult/child interactions, relations between the home and program, and developmental evaluation of children.

National Association for the Education of Young Children, "Position Statement on Developmentally Appropriate Practice in Early Childhood Programs Serving Children from Birth Through Age 8," *Young Children* (September 1986). Article excerpted by Barbara L. Andress with permission.

Defining Developmental Appropriateness

The concept of developmental appropriateness has two dimensions; age appropriateness and individual appropriateness:

- Age appropriateness. Human development research indicates that there are universal, predictable sequences of growth and change that occur in children during the first nine years of life. These predictable changes occur in all domains of development—physical, emotional, social, and cognitive. Knowledge of typical development of children within the age span served by the program provides a framework from which teachers prepare the learning environment and plan appropriate experiences.
- Individual appropriateness. Each child is a unique person with an individual pattern and timing of growth, as well as individual personality, learning style, and family background.

The following material illustrates practices that are both age appropriate and individually appropriate. Teachers can use child-development knowledge to identify the range of appropriate behaviors, activities, and materials for a specific age-group. This knowledge is used in conjunction with understanding about individual children's growth patterns, strengths, interests, and experiences to design the most appropriate learning environment. Although the content of the curriculum is determined by many factors such as tradition, the subject matter of the disciplines, social or cultural values, and parental desires, for the content and teaching strategies to be developmentally appropriate they must be age appropriate and individually appropriate.

Children's play is a primary vehicle for and indicator of their mental growth. Play enables children to progress along the developmental sequence from sensorimotor intelligence of infancy to preoperational thought in the preschool years to the concrete operational thinking exhib-

ited by primary children. In addition to its role in cognitive development, play also serves important functions in children's physical, emotional, and social development. Therefore, child-initiated, child-directed, teacher-supported play is an essential component of developmentally appropriate practice.

Guidelines for Developmentally Appropriate Practice

Curriculum. A developmentally appropriate curriculum for young children is planned to be appropriate for the age span of the children within the group and is implemented with attention to the different needs, interests, and developmental levels of those individual children.

- *Developmentally appropriate curriculum provides for all areas of a child's development: physical, emotional, social, and cognitive through an integrated approach.*

Realistic curriculum goals for children should address all of these ages in age-appropriate ways. Children's learning does not occur in narrowly defined subject areas; their development and learning are integrated. Any activity that stimulates one dimension of development and learning affects other dimensions as well.

- *Appropriate curriculum planning is based on teachers' observations and recordings of each child's special interests and developmental progress.*

Realistic curriculum goals and plans are based on regular assessment of individual needs, strengths, and interest. Curriculum is based on both age-appropriate and individual-appropriate information. For example, children's family and cultural backgrounds—including expressive styles, ways of interacting, play, and games—are used to broaden the curriculum for all children.

• *Curriculum planning emphasizes learning as an interactive process. Teachers prepare the environment for children to learn through active exploration and interaction with adults, other children, and materials.*

The process of interacting with materials and people results in learning. Finished products or "correct" solutions that conform to adult standards are not very accurate criteria for judging whether learning has occurred. Much of young children's learning takes place when they direct their own play activities. During play, children feel successful when they engage in a task they have defined for themselves, such as finding their way through an obstacle course with a friend or pouring water into and out of various containers. Such learning should not be inhibited by adult-established concepts of completion, achievement, and failure. Activities should be designed to concentrate on furthering emerging skills through creative activity and intense involvement.

Children need years of play with real objects and events before they are able to understand the meaning of symbols such as letters and numbers. Learning takes place as young children touch, manipulate, and experiment with things and interact with people.

Workbooks, worksheets, coloring books, and adult-made models of art products for children to copy are not appropriate for young children, especially for those younger than six.

Basic learning materials and activities for an appropriate curriculum include sand, water, clay, and accessories to use with them; table unit and hollow blocks; puzzles with varying numbers of pieces; many types of games; a variety of small manipulative toys; dramatic play props and items to explore; a changing selection of appropriate and aesthetically pleasing books and recordings; supplies of paper, water-based paint, markers, and other materials for creative expression; large muscle equipment; field trips; classroom responsibilities, such as helping with routines; and positive interactions and problem-solving opportunities with other children and adults.

• *Programs provide for a wider range of developmental interest and abilities than the chronological age range of the group would suggest. Adults are prepared to meet the needs of children who exhibit unusual interests and skills outside the normal developmental range.*

Activities and equipment should be provided for a chronological age range that in many cases is at least twelve months. However, the normal developmental age range in any group may be as much as two years. Some mainstreamed situations will demand a wider range of expectations. When the developmental age range of a group is more than eighteen months, the need increases for a large variety of furnishings, equipment, and teaching strategies. The complexity of materials should also reflect the age span of the group.

• *Teachers provide a variety of activities and materials; teachers increase the difficulty, complexity, and challenge of an activity as children are involved with it and as children develop understanding and skills.*

As children work with materials or activities, teachers listen, observe, and interpret children's behavior. Teachers can then facilitate children's involvement and learning by asking questions, making suggestions, or adding more complex material or ideas to a situation. Examples of developmentally appropriate learning activities for various age groups include:

For infants and toddlers: Infants and toddlers learn by experiencing the environment through their senses (seeing, hearing, tasting, smelling, and feeling), by physically moving around, and through social interaction. Nonmobile infants absorb and organize a great deal of information about the world around them, so adults talk and sing with them about what is happening and bring them objects to observe and manipulate. At times adults carry nonmobile infants around the environment to show them interesting events and people. Mobile infants and toddlers increasingly use toys, language, and other learning materials in their play.

Adults play a vital socialization role with infants and toddlers. Warm, positive relationships with adults help infants develop a sense of trust in the world and feelings of competence. The trusted adult becomes the secure base from which the mobile infant or toddler explores the environment.

Important independence skills are acquired during these years. The most appropriate teaching technique for this age group is to give ample opportunities for children to use self-initiated repetition to practice newly acquired skills and to experience feelings of autonomy and success. Infants will bat at, grasp, bang, or drop their toys. Patience is essential as a toddler struggles to put on a sweater. Imitation, hiding, and naming games are also important for learning at this age. Realistic toys will enable children to engage in increasingly complex types of play.

Two-year-olds learn to produce language rapidly. They need simple books, pictures, puzzles, and music, and time and space for active play such as jumping, running, and dancing. Toddlers acquire social skills, but in groups there should be several of the same toy because egocentric toddlers are not yet able to understand the concept of sharing.

For three-, four-, and five-year-olds: Curriculum for three-year-olds should emphasize language, activity, and movement, with major emphasis on large muscle activity. Appropriate activities include dramatic play, wheel toys and climbers, puzzles and blocks, and opportunities to talk and listen to simple stories.

Four-year-olds enjoy a greater variety of experiences and more small-motor activities like cutting with scissors, creating art, using manipulatives, and cooking. They are more able to concentrate and remember as well as recognize objects by shape, color, or size. Four-year-olds develop basic math concepts and problem-solving skills.

Some four-year-olds and most five-year-olds combine ideas into more complex relations (for example, number concepts such as one-to-one correspondence) and have growing memory capacity and fine motor physical skills. Some four-year-olds and most five-year-olds display a growing interest in the functional aspects of written language, such as recognizing meaningful words and trying to write their own names. Activities designed solely to teach the alphabet, phonics, and penmanship are much less appropriate for this age group than providing a print-rich environment that stimulates the development of language and literacy skills in a meaningful context.

Curriculum for four- and five-year-olds can expand beyond the child's immediate experiences of self, home, and family to include special events and trips. Five-year-olds develop interest in community and the world outside their own. They also use motor skills well, even daringly, and show increasing ability to pay attention for longer times and in large groups if the topic is meaningful.

• *Adults provide opportunities for children to choose from among a variety of activities, materials, and equipment and provide time to explore through active involvement. Adults facilitate children's engagement with materials and activities and extend the child's learning by asking questions or making suggestions that stimulate children's thinking.*

Children of all ages need uninterrupted periods of time to become involved in, investigate, select, and persist at activities. The teacher's role in child-chosen activity is to prepare the environment with stimulating, challenging activity choices and then to facilitate children's engagement. In developmentally appropriate programs, adults:

- provide a rich variety of activities and materials from which to choose;
- offer children the choice to participate in a small group or in a solitary activity;
- assist and guide children who are not yet able to enjoy and easily use child-choice activity periods; and
- provide opportunities for child-initiated, child-directed practice of skills as a self-chosen activity.

• *Multicultural and nonsexist experiences, materials, and equipment should be provided for children of all ages to:*

  • enhance each child's self-concept and esteem;

  • support the integrity of the child's family;

  • enhance the child's learning processes in both the home and the early childhood program by strengthening ties;

  • extend experiences of children and their families to include knowledge of the ways of others, especially those who share the community; and

  • enrich the lives of all participants with respectful acceptance and appreciation of differences and similarities among them.

Multicultural experiences should not be limited to a celebration of holidays and should include information on foods, music, family life, shelter, and other aspects common to all cultures.

• *Adults provide a balance of rest and active movement for children through the program day.*

For infants and toddlers, naps and quiet activities such as listening to rhymes and music provide periodic rest from the intense physical exploration that is characteristic of this age-group. The balance between active and quiet activity should be maintained throughout the day by alternating activities.

• *Outdoor experiences should be provided for children of all ages.*

Outdoor time is an integral part of the curriculum and requires planning; it is not simply a time for children to release pent-up energy.

Adult-Child Interaction. The developmental appropriateness of an early childhood program is most apparent in the interactions between adults and children. Developmentally appropriate interactions are based on adults' knowledge and expectations of age-appropriate behavior in children balanced by adult's awareness of individual differences among children.

• *Adults respond quickly and directly to children's needs, desires, and messages and adapt their responses to children's differing styles and abilities.*

Adults hold and touch infants frequently; talk and sing to infants in a soothing, friendly voice; smile and maintain eye contact with infants. For toddlers and two-year-olds, adults remain close by, giving attention and physical comfort as needed. Adults repeat children's words, paraphrase, or use synonyms or actions to help assure toddlers that they are understood. As children get older, adult responses are characterized by less physical communication and more verbal responsiveness, although immediacy is still important. With all age-groups, adults should be aware of the powerful influence of modeling and other nonverbal communication; adults' actions should be compatible with their verbal messages and confirm that children understand their messages.

• *Adults provide many varied opportunities for children to communicate.*

Children acquire communication skills through hearing and using language, and as adults listen and respond to what children say. Communication skills grow out of the desire to use language to express needs, insights, and excitement, and to solve problems. Listening experiences—when there is something meaningful to listen to—can enrich language learning. One-on-one exchanges are critical through the early years. Children's questions, and their responses to questions, particularly open-ended questions, provide valuable information about the individual's level of thinking.

• *Adults facilitate a child's successful completion of tasks by providing support, focused attention, physical proximity, and verbal encouragement. Adults recognize that children learn from trial and error and that children's misconceptions reflect their developing thoughts.*

Children learn from their own mistakes. Adults can examine the problem with the child and, if appropriate, encourage the child to try again or to find alternatives.

• *Teachers are alert to signs of undue stress in children's behavior, and aware of appropriate stress-reducing activities and techniques.*

Formal, inappropriate instructional techniques are a source of stress for young children. When children exhibit stress-related behavior, teachers should examine the program to ensure that expectations are appropriate and are not placing excessive demands on children.

• *Adults facilitate the development of self-esteem by expressing respect for, acceptance of, and comfort with children, regardless of the child's behavior.*

Understanding behavior that is not unusual for young children, such as messiness, interest in body parts and genital differences, crying and resistance, aggression, and later infraction of rules and truth, is the basis for appropriate guidance of young children. Developmentally appropriate guidance helps children develop self-control and the ability to make better decisions in the future.

• *Adults facilitate the development of self-control in children.*

Children learn self-control when adults treat them with dignity and use discipline techniques such as:
  • guiding children by setting clear, consistent, fair limits for classroom behavior; or in the case of older children, helping them to set their own limits;
  • valuing mistakes as learning opportunities;
  • redirecting children to more acceptable behavior or activity;
  • listening when children talk about their feelings and frustrations;

  • guiding children to resolve conflicts and modeling skills that help children solve their own problems; and
  • patiently reminding children of rules and their rationale as needed.

• *Adults are responsible for all children under their supervision at all times and plan for increasing independence as children acquire skills.*

Adults must constantly and closely supervise and attend every child younger than the age of three. They must be close enough to touch infants when awake, catch a climbing toddler before she hits the ground, be aware of every move of a two-year-old, and be close enough to offer another toy when two-year-olds have difficulty sharing. Adults must be responsible for three- to five-year-old children at all times, in an environment sufficiently open to permit it.

Relations Between Home and Program. To achieve individually appropriate programs for young children, early childhood teachers must work in partnership with families and communicate regularly with children's parents.

• *Parents have both the right and the responsibility to share in decisions about their children's care and education. Parents should be encouraged to observe and participate. Teachers are responsible for establishing and maintaining frequent contacts with families.*

• *Teachers share child-development knowledge, insights, and resources as part of regular communication and conferences with family members.*

• *Teachers, parents, agencies, programs, and consultants who may have educational responsibility for the child at different times should, with family participation, share developmental information about children as they pass from one level or program to another.*

Continuity of educational experience is critical to supporting development. Such continuity results from communication both horizontally, as children change programs within a given year, and vertically, as children move on to other settings.

Developmental Evaluation of Children. Assessment of each individual child's development and learning is essential for planning and implementing developmentally appropriate programs, but should be used with caution to prevent discrimination against individuals and to ensure accuracy. Accurate testing can only be achieved with reliable, valid instruments and such instruments developed for use with young children are extremely rare. In the absence of valid instruments, testing is not valuable. Therefore, assessment of young children should rely heavily on the results of observations of their development and descriptive data.

Essential Policies for Developmentally Appropriate Programs

• *Early childhood teachers should have college-level, specialized preparation in early childhood education/child development. Teachers in early childhood programs, regardless of credentialed status, should be encouraged and supported to obtain and maintain current knowledge of child development and its application to early childhood educational practice.*

• *Early childhood teachers should have practical experiences teaching the age-group.*

• *Implementation of developmentally appropriate early childhood programs requires limiting the size of the group and providing sufficient numbers of adults to provide individualized and age-appropriate care and education.*

Resources

These references contain information on both laboratory and clinical classroom research to document the broad-based literature that forms the foundation for sound practice in early childhood education.

Almy, M. *The Early Childhood Educator at Work.* New York: McGraw-Hill, 1975.

Almy, M. "Day Care and Early Childhood Education." In *Daycare: Scientific and Social Policy Issues,* edited by E. Zigler and E. Gordon. Boston: Auburn House, 1982, 476–95.

Asher, S. R., P. D. Renshaw, and S. Hymel. "Peer Relations and the Development of Social Skills." In *The Young Child: Reviews of Research.* Vol. 3, edited by S. G. Moore and C. R. Cooper. Washington, DC: NAEYC, 1982, 137–58.

Baker, K. R., P. Gardner, and B. Mahler. *Early Childhood Programs: A Laboratory for Human Relationships.* 8th ed. New York: Rinehart & Winston, 1986.

Biber, B. *Early Education and Psychological Development.* New Haven: Yale University Press, 1984.

Brazelton, T. B. "Cementing Family Relationships Through Child Care." In *The Infants We Care For.* rev. ed., edited by L. Dittman. Washington, DC: NAEYC, 1984.

Cazden, C., ed. *Language in Early Childhood Education.* rev. ed. Washington, DC: NAEYC, 1981.

Cohen, D. H., V. Stern, and N. Balaban. *Observing and Recording the Behavior of Young Children.* 3rd ed. New York: Teachers College Press, Columbia University, 1983.

Coopersmith, S. "Building Self-Esteem in the Classroom." *Developing Motivation in Young Children,* edited by S. Coopersmith. San Francisco: Albion, 1975.

Cratty, B. "Motor Development in Early Childhood: Critical Issues for Researchers in the 1980s." In *Handbook of Research in Early Childhood Education,* edited by B. Spodek. New York: Free Press, 1982.

Croft, D. J. *Parents and Teachers: A Resource Book for Home, School, and Community Relations.* Belmont, CA: Wadsworth, 1979.

Curtis, S. "New Views on Movement Development and Implications for Curriculum in Early Childhood Education." In *Early Childhood Curriculum: A Review of Current Research*, edited by C. Seefeldt. New York: Teachers College Press, Columbia University, 1986.

Davidson, L. "Preschool Children's Tonal Knowledge: Antecedents of Scale." In *The Young Child and Music: Contemporary Principles in Child Development and Music Education. Proceedings of the Music in Early Childhood Conference*, edited by J. Boswell. Reston, VA: Music Educators National Conference, 1985, 25–40.

Dittmann, L. *The Infants We Care For*. rev. ed. Washington, DC: NAEYC, 1984.

Dreikurs, R., B. Grunwald, and S. Pepper. *Maintaining Sanity in the Classroom*. New York: Harper & Row, 1982.

Elkind, D. "Formal Education and Early Childhood Education: An Essential Difference." *Phi Delta Kappan* (May 1986): 631–36.

Erikson, E. *Childhood and Society*. New York: Norton, 1950.

Evans, E. D. "Children's Aesthetics." In *Current Topics in Early Childhood Education*. Vol. 5, edited by L. G. Katz. Norwood, NJ: Ablex, 1984, 73–104.

Feeney, S., and R. Chun. "Research in Review. Effective Teachers of Young Children." *Young Children* 41, no. 1 (1985): 47–52.

Fein, G. "Play and the Acquisition of Symbols." In *Current Topics in Early Childhood Education*. Vol. 2, edited by L. Katz. Norwood, NJ: Ablex, 1979.

Fein, G., and M. Rivkin, eds. *The Young Child at Play: Reviews of Research*. Vol. 4. Washington, DC: NAEYC, 1986.

Ferreiro, E., and A. Teberosky. *Literacy Before Schooling*. Exeter, NH: Heinemann, 1982.

Forman, G., and D. Kuschner. *The Child's Construction of Knowledge: Piaget for Teaching Children*. Washington, DC: NAEYC, 1983.

Fromberg, D. "Play." In *Early Childhood Curriculum: A Review of Current Research*, edited by C. Seefeldt. New York: Teachers College Press, Columbia University, 1986.

Frost, J. L., and B. L. Klein. *Children's Play and Playgrounds*. Austin, TX: Playgrounds International, 1979.

Gazda, G. M. *Human Relations Development: A Manual for Educators*. Boston: Allyn & Bacon, 1973.

Genishi, C. "Acquiring Language and Communicative Competence." In *Early Childhood Curriculum: A Review of Current Research*, edited by C. Seefeldt. New York: Teachers College Press, Columbia University, 1986.

Gerber, M. "What Is Appropriate Curriculum for Infants and Toddlers?" In *Infants: Their Social Environments*, edited by B. Weissbourd and J. Musick. Washington, DC: NAEYC, 1982.

Gilbert, J. P. "Motoric Music Skill Development in Young Children: A Longitudinal Investigation." *Psychology of Music* 9, no. 1 (1981): 21–24.

Goffin, S., and C. Tull. "Problem Solving: Encouraging Active Learning." *Young Children* 40, no. 3 (1985): 28–32.

Gonzales-Mena, J., and D. W. Eyer. *Infancy and Caregiving*. Palo Alto, CA: Mayfield, 1980.

Goodman, W., and L. Goodman. "Measuring Young Children." In *Handbook of Research in Early Childhood Education*, edited by B. Spodek. New York: Free Press, 1982.

Gordon, T. *Parent Effectiveness Training*. New York: Wyden, 1970.

Gordon, T. *Teacher Effectiveness Training*. New York: McKay, 1975.

Gottfried, A. "Research in Review. Intrinsic Motivation in Young Children." *Young Children* 39, no. 1 (1983): 64–73.

Greenberg, M. "Research in Music in Early Childhood Education: A Survey with Recommendations." *Council for Research in Music Education* 45 (1976): 1–20.

Greenspan, S., and N. T. Greenspan. *First Feelings: Milestones in the Emotional Development of Your Baby and Child*. New York: Viking, 1985.

Griffin, E. F. *The Island of Childhood: Education in the Special World of Nursery School*. New York:

Teachers College Press, Columbia University, 1982.

Hendrick, J. *Total Learning: Curriculum for the Young Child.* 2d ed. Columbus, OH: Merrill, 1986.

Herron, R., and B. Sutton-Smith. *Child's Play.* New York: Wiley, 1974.

Hoffman, M. L. "Moral Internalization, Parental Power, and the Nature of Parent-Child Interaction." *Developmental Psychology,* II (1975): 228–39.

Honig, A. S. "The Young Child and You—Learning Together." *Young Children* 35, no. 4 (1980): 2–10.

Honig, A. S. "What Are the Needs of Infants?" *Young Children* 37, no. 1 (1981): 3–10.

Honig, A. S. "Parent Involvement in Early Childhood Education." In *Handbook of Research in Early Childhood Education,* edited by B. Spodek. New York: Free Press, 1982.

Honig, A. S. "Research in Review. Compliance, Control, and Discipline." Parts 1 and 2. *Young Children* 40, no. 2 (1985): 50–58; 40, no. 3 (1985): 47–52.

Honig, A. S. "Research in Review. Stress and Coping Children." Parts 1 and 2. *Young Children* 41, no. 4 (1986): 50–63; 41, no. 5 (1986): 47–59.

Kamii, C. *Number in Preschool and Kindergarten.* Washington, DC: NAEYC, 1982.

Kamii, C. "Leading Primary Education Toward Excellence: Beyond Worksheets and Drill." *Young Children* 40, no. 6 (1985): 3–9.

Kamii, C., and R. DeVries. *Group Games in Early Education.* Washington, DC: NAEYC, 1980.

Kamii, C., and L. Lee-Katz. "Physics in Early Childhood Education: A Piagetian Approach." *Young Children* 34, no. 4 (1979): 4–9.

Katz, L. "Mothering and Teaching: Some Significant Distinctions." In *Current Topics in Early Childhood Education.* Vol. 3, edited by L. Katz. Norwood, NJ: Ablex, 1980, 47–64.

Kitano, M. "Young Gifted Children: Strategies for Preschool Teachers." *Young Children* 37, no. 4 (1982): 14–24.

Kline, L. W. *Learning to Read, Teaching to Read.* Newark, DE: LWK Enterprises, 1985.

Kobak, D. "Teaching Children to Care." *Children Today* 8 (1979): 6–7, 34–35.

Kohlberg, L., and R. Mayer. "Development as the Aim of Education." *Harvard Educational Review* 42 (1972): 449–96.

Kopp, C. B. "Antecedents of Self-Regulation: A Developmental Perspective." *Developmental Psychology* 18 (1982): 199–214.

Kuczynski, L. "Reasoning, Prohibitions, and Motivations for Compliance." *Developmental Psychology* 19 (1983): 126–34.

Languis, M., T. Sanders, and S. Tipps. *Brain and Learning: Directions in Early Childhood Education.* Washington, DC: NAEYC, 1980.

Lasky, L., and R. Mukerji. *Art: Basic for Young Children.* Washington, DC: NAEYC, 1980.

Lay-Dopyera, M., and J. Dopyera. "Strategies for Teaching." In *Early Childhood Curriculum: A Review of Current Research,* edited by C. Seefeldt. New York: Teachers College Press, Columbia University, 1986.

Lickona, T. *Raising Good Children.* New York: Bantam, 1983.

Lightfoot, S. *Worlds Apart: Relationships Between Families and Schools.* New York: Basic, 1978.

McAfee, O. "Research Report. Circle Time: Getting Past 'Two Little Pumpkins.'" *Young Children* 40, no. 6 (1986): 24–29.

McCracken, J. B., ed. *Helping Young Children Cope with Stress.* Washington, DC: NAEYC, 1986.

McDonald, D. T. *Music in Our Lives: The Early Years.* Washington, DC: NAEYC, 1979.

Meisels, S. *Developmental Screening in Early Childhood.* Washington, DC: NAEYC, 1985.

Miller, C. S. "Building Self-Control: Discipline for Young Children." *Young Children* 40, no. 1 (1984): 15–19.

Montessori, M. *The Montessori Method.* Cambridge, MA: Robert Bentley, 1964.

Moore, S. "Prosocial Behavior in the Early Years: Parent and Peer Influences." In *Handbook of Research in Early Childhood Education,* edited by B. Spodek. New York: Free Press, 1982.

Mussen, P. and N. Eisenberg-Bert. *Roots of Caring, Sharing, and Helping: The Development of Prosocial Behavior in Children*. San Francisco: Freeman, 1977.

NAEYC. *Early Childhood Teacher Education Guidelines for Four- and Five-Year Programs*. Washington, DC: NAEYC, 1984.

NAEYC. *Accreditation Criteria and Procedures of the National Academy of Early Childhood Programs*. Washington, DC: NAEYC, 1984.

National Institute of Education. *Becoming a Nation of Readers: The Report of the Commission on Reading*. Washington, DC: U. S. Department of Education, 1984.

Piaget, J. *The Psychology of Intelligence*. London: Routledge & Kegan Paul, 1950.

Piaget, J. *The Origins of Intelligence in Children*. Translated by M. Cook. New York: Norton, 1952. (Original work published 1936.)

Piaget, J. *Science of Education and the Psychology of the Child*. rev. ed. New York: Viking, 1972. (Original work published 1965.)

Powell, D. "Effects of Program Approaches and Teaching Practices." *Young Children* 41, no. 6. (1986): 60–67.

Ramsey, P. G. "Beyond `Ten Little Indians' and Turkeys: Alternative Approaches to Thanksgiving." *Young Children* 34, no. 6 (1979): 28–32, 49–52.

Ramsey, P. G. "Multicultural Education in Early Childhood." *Young Children* 37, no. 2 (1982): 13–24.

Read, K. H., P. Gardner, and B. Mahler. *Early Childhood Programs: A Laboratory for Human Relationships*. 8th ed. New York: Holt, Rinehart & Winston, 1986.

Riley, S. S. *How to Generate Values in Young Children: Integrity, Honesty, Individuality, Self-Confidence*. Washington, DC: NAEYC, 1984.

Rogers, D. L., and D. D. Ross. "Encouraging Positive Social Interaction Among Young Children." *Young Children* 41, no. 3 (1986): 12–17.

Rubin, K., and B. Everett. "Social Perspective-Taking in Young Children." In *The Young Child: Reviews of Research*, edited by S. G. Moore and C. R. Cooper. Vol. 3. Washington, DC: NAEYC, 1982.

Ruoop, R., J. Travers, F. Glantz, and C. Coelen. *Children at the Center. Final Report of the National Day Care Study*. Vol. 1. Cambridge, MA: Abt Associates, 1979.

Sackoff, E., and R. Hart. "Toys: Research and Applications." *Children's Environments Quarterly* (Summer 1984): 1–2.

Saracho, O., and B. Spodek, eds. *Understanding the Multicultural Experience in Early Childhood Education*. Washington, DC: NAEYC, 1983.

Schacter, F. F., and A. A. Strage. "Adults' Talk and Children's Language Development." In *The Young Child: Reviews of Research*. Vol. 3, edited by S. G. Moore and C. R. Cooper. Washington, DC: NAEYC, 1982, 79–96.

Schaffer, H. R. *The Child's Entry into a Social World*. Orlando, FL: Academic, 1984.

Schickedanz, J. *More Than the ABCs: The Early Stages of Reading and Writing*. Washington, DC: NAEYC, 1986.

Schickedanz, J., D. I. Schickedanz, and P. D. Forsyth. *Toward Understanding Children*. Boston: Little and Brown, 1982.

Seefeldt, C. "The Visual Arts." In *The Early Childhood Curriculum: A Review of Current Research*, edited by C. Seefeldt. New York: Teachers College Press, Columbia University, 1986.

Shure, M. B., and G. Spivack. *Problem-Solving Techniques in Childrearing*. San Francisco: Jossey-Bass, 1978.

Smith, C. A., and D. E. Davis, "Teaching Children Non-Sense." *Young Children* 34, no. 3 (1976): 4–11.

Smith, F. *Understanding Reading*. New York: Holt, Rinehart & Winston, 1982.

Smith, N. *Experience and Art: Teaching Children to Paint*. New York: Teachers College Press, Columbia University, 1983.

Souweine, J., S. Crimmins, and C. Mazel. *Mainstreaming: Ideas for Teaching Young Children*. Washington, DC: NAEYC, 1981.

Sparling, J. *Learning Games for the First Three Years*. New York: Walker, 1984.

Spodek, B. *Teaching in the Early Years.* 3rd ed. Englewood Cliffs, NJ: Prentice Hall, 1985.

Sponseller, D. "Play and Early Education." In *Handbook of Research in Early Childhood Education,* edited by B. Spodek. New York: Free Press, 1982.

Sprung, B. *Perspectives on Non-Sexist Early Childhood Education.* New York: Teachers College Press, Columbia University, 1978.

Sroufe, L. A. "The Coherence of Individual Development." *American Psychologist* 34 (1979): 834–41.

Standards of Educational and Psychological Testing. Washington, DC: American Psychological Association, American Educational Research Association, and National Council on Measurement in Education, 1985.

Stewart, I. S. "The Real World of Teaching Two-Year-Old Children." *Young Children* 37, no. 5 (1982): 3–13.

Stone, J. G. *A Guide to Discipline.* rev. ed. Washington, DC: NAEYC, 1978.

Uphoff, J. K., and J. Gilmore. *Educational Leadership* 43 (September 1985): 86–90.

Veach, D. M. "Choice with Responsibility." *Young Children* 32, no. 4 (1977): 22–25.

Wallinga, C. R., and A. L. Sweaney. "A Sense of *Real* Accomplishment: Young Children as Productive Family Members." *Young Children* 41, no. 1 (1985): 3–9.

Warren, R. M. *Caring: Supporting Children's Growth.* Washington, DC: NAEYC, 1977.

Weber, E. *Ideas Influencing Early Childhood Education: A Theoretical Analysis.* New York: Teachers College Press, Columbia University, 1984.

Weissbourd, B. "Supporting Parents as People." In *Infants: Their Social Environments,* edited by B. Weissbourd and J. Musick. Washington, DC: NAEYC, 1981.

Wellman, H. M. "The Foundations of Knowledge: Concept Development in the Young Child." In *The Young Child: Reviews of Research.* Vol. 3, edited by S. G. Moore and C. R. Cooper. Washington, DC: NAEYC, 1982, 115–34.

Willert, M., and C. Kamii. "Reading in Kindergarten: Direct Versus Indirect Teaching." *Young Children* 40, no. 4 (1985): 3–9.

Willis, A., and H. Ricciuti. *A Good Beginning for Babies: Guidelines for Group Care.* Washington, DC: NAEYC, 1975.

Wolfgang, C. H., and C. D. Glickman. *Solving Discipline Problems.* Boston: Allyn & Bacon, 1980.

Yarrow, M. R., P. M. Scott, and C. Z. Waxler. "Learning Concern for Others." *Developmental Psychology* 8 (1973): 240–60.

Yarrow, M. R., and C. Z. Waxler. "Dimensions and Correlates of Prosocial Behavior in Young Children." *Child Development* 47 (1976): 118–25.

Zavitkovsky, D., K. R. Baker, J. R. Berlfein, and M. Almy. *Listen to the Children.* Washington, DC: NAEYC, 1986.

Ziegler, P. "Saying Good-Bye to Pre-School." *Young Children* 40, no. 3 (1985): 11–15.

Barbara L. Andress is professor emeritus in the school of music at Arizona State University—Tempe. She is an active author, speaker/clinician, and a current member of the MENC Task Force on Music in Early Childhood.

To know how the child develops is important. To know how the child can and should interact with music at the various stages of development is our role as music educators. John Feierabend focuses on the importance of the young child's *musical* development. He explores how music permeates the child's daily curricular experiences and explores the concepts of music for music's sake, music as a separate intelligence, musical aptitude, and routes to musical achievement. He well states that "caring about the whole child means caring about arts education."

Music in Early Childhood

❖

BY JOHN FEIERABEND

t should not come as a surprise that early training in the arts can make a marked difference in the later development of an individual. Although this is being confirmed by an increasing number of research studies, most parents and teachers remain uninformed on the importance of readiness training in the arts.

Music, perhaps more than the other arts, has traditionally been integrated into early childhood curricula. Early childhood specialists have embraced the integration of music into their curricula and rationalized its use because of the extramusical benefits in the area of social, cognitive, motor, affective, and creative development. In addition, standard developmental stages are often measured by testing a child's ability to perform tasks easily learned through musical activities. For example, in the *Developmental Profile II*, physical development is measured on the basis of hopping forward on one foot, jumping rope, or whistling a recognizable tune—all activities naturally explored in children's singing games.[1] The profile's social development subtest measures a child's ability to clap hands (pat-a-cake) or to take turns playing games. Its academic development subtest measures cogni-

tive development through such tasks as rhyming words, and communication development is assessed through such things as the ability to repeat all or parts of nursery rhymes, sing songs, rhyme words, and create original songs. What better way do we have to assist these developmental abilities than to provide guided musical experiences during the formative years?

A recent educational trend is the "whole language" approach to language skills in the early elementary years.[2] The idea is that speaking, reading, and writing are most naturally nurtured by using words and concepts from the child's experience without overemphasizing correct spelling or grammar. The emphasis is on supporting self-expression, gradually working toward refinement in much the same way that early speaking skills naturally evolve from enthusiastic attempts to refined precision. To follow this philosophy in music, we would use songs that have traditionally emerged from the child's world. The use of traditional children's folk songs and rhymes ensures a natural flow of musical language and textual content relevant to the young child's interests. A further support for the use of traditional children's folk songs and rhymes can be found in the recent interest in cultural literacy—the theory that all educated people who

John Feierabend, "Music in Early Childhood," *Design for Arts in Education* 91, no. 6 (July/August 1990): 15–20. Reprinted with permission of the Helen Dwight Reid Education Foundation. Published by Heldref Publications, 1319 Eighteenth Street, Washington, DC 20036. Copyright © 1990.

share the same culture should have a common body of knowledge.[3] Is an individual tuned into the American culture if he or she has not shared a standard repertory of traditional American children's songs and rhymes—songs like "Twinkle, Twinkle" and "The Eensy Weensy Spider"? Folk songs from other cultures might also be included to begin fostering multicultural insights.

Music for Music's Sake

Whether the music is used to reinforce the whole-language approach; to nurture cultural literacy; or to assist in the natural development of social, cognitive, motor, affective, or creative skills, one basic prerequisite remains: Can the child be successful with music?

If music activities are to be the vehicles to facilitate "extramusical" learnings, care must be given to develop primary music skills: comfortable singing and rhythmic moving. Furthermore, music must not be justified solely for its ability to facilitate skill development in other areas. Nurturing music skills should be considered essential in early childhood simply because of the richness it brings to one's life.

Our society assumes certain musical behavior from all of us throughout our adult lives. We are expected to dance at weddings, cheer at sporting events while clapping hands in time with the crowd, sing "Happy Birthday" to friends and relatives, or share a lullaby with an infant. Although all people should have those minimum musical competencies, some will be more deeply involved with music as consumers of recorded and live music, while others will become performing musicians. Regardless of our ultimate level of involvement with music, the success of our musical experiences may depend on the musical nurturing we received during our preschool years.

Success in singing and moving to music involves a type of intelligence independent of other intellectual skills. Early childhood specialists most commonly consider music activities in light of the ways they benefit extramusical skills rather than for the development of musical skills for their own sake. In his thought-provoking *Frames of Mind*, however, Howard Gardner helps us understand the importance of recognizing the variety of separate intelligences each of us possesses: linguistic, logical-mathematical, musical, spatial, bodily-kinesthetic, interpersonal, and intrapersonal.[4] Gardner challenges us to nurture all our capabilities, including musical intelligence. Instead of judging overall intelligence by considering only one or two areas, Gardner suggests that we each have our own profile of strengths and weaknesses among all seven intelligences. If one person is exceptionally intelligent in one or two of the seven (say, music and bodily-kinesthetic) and only average in the others, is such a person any less intelligent than another who might have two other exceptional intelligences (for example, linguistic and logical-mathematical)?

Until recently, society has not placed equal emphasis on each of the seven intelligences. Many educational psychologists are awaiting with great interest the results of "Project Zero," a model school in Boston based on Gardner's theories. Students are involved in a schedule that places equal emphasis on each of the seven intellectual realms. Because this curriculum was only recently put in place, no results have yet been reported. The concept, however, is already being replicated in several other locations. Directors of early childhood programs might wish to consider adopting the "project zero" concept for their preschool children.

Music as a Separate Intelligence

The theory of multiple intelligences suggests that music is an independent intelligence that may be helped or hindered by the influence of parents and early childhood specialists. According to Gardner, all children deserve to have all seven intelligences nourished so that they may function at their full potential. If any are overlooked, essential learning stages may be missed in early childhood and the potential intelligence may diminish.

This concept of diminishing intelligence has been supported by the research of Edwin Gordon at Temple University. In 1965, Gordon began to explore music intelligence through the development of a music aptitude test, Musical Aptitude Profile (MAP).[5] Designed for students ages nine to eighteen, the test measures the ability to retain a short melody "in your mind" and then compare it with a second melody. Gordon defines the ability to hear music that is not physically present as "audiation" and determines the level of musical aptitude by the ability "to audiate." He found that each individual tested rarely scored similarly on the tonal and rhythmic subtests. In general, those who score superbly on one part of the test will have average scores on the other part. According to Gordon, we are each stronger in one kind of music intelligence than in the other. As Gordon retested students as they progressed through junior high and high school, he discovered that they retained the same levels of audiation ability. A twelve-year-old student who performed at the fiftieth percentile would be likely to perform at the fiftieth percentile at eighteen. Our audiation as adults resembles our audiation as nine-year-olds. Furthermore, it appears that participation in a music ensemble such as band, orchestra, or choir has little effect on audiation ability after age nine. While students may learn to perform better and develop musical coordination skills through the school years, they cannot actually enhance their basic aptitude for mentally retaining tonal or rhythmic patterns. More recent research on children younger than nine years old produced more startling findings.

Music Aptitude

In 1978, Gordon developed a simplified version of MAP for children between the ages of five and nine. The Primary Measures of Music Audiation (PMMA) contains two parts: one measures tonal audiation and one measures rhythmic audiation.[6] When he administered the tests in subsequent years to the same students between the ages of five and nine, Gordon discovered that music audiation scores would decline if the children did not receive musical stimulation. In school districts where there was no general music in the elementary curriculum, or where the program did not stress singing and rhythmic moving, Gordon consistently found similar results. Of great importance was the finding that the greatest loss in audiation occurred between the ages of five and six. There was a significant, though less severe, decline in audiation scores between the ages of six and seven. Audiation scores continued to decline each year the student aged, but less significantly. From eight to nine there was only a slight loss in audiation scores, and at nine music audiation stabilized. In one study, Gordon tested students who began public school music in the second grade (approximately at age seven). As before, students' scores declined between the ages of five and seven. Scores increased slightly from ages seven to eight, and even less from eight to nine. The audiation scores that then stabilized at age nine were slightly higher than those at age eight but noticeably lower than at age five. It appears that the longer the delay in music stimulation in the form of singing and rhythmic moving, the more the ability to audiate can be lost and the less will be regained.

Although there is currently no test to measure music aptitude in children younger than five years, there is a clear trend in Gordon's research. If the greatest loss in music audiation occurs between the ages of five and six, what happens between the ages of four and five or from birth to five? Children are probably born with their own level of music intelligences that begin to atrophy unless supported by a musical environment. If children have not experienced singing and rhythmic moving at home, by the time they reach kindergarten their music aptitudes have probably declined significantly. If they are given a nurturing environment starting in kindergarten, their music aptitude scores can increase until age nine. Aptitude scores can also show the greatest increase between the ages of five and six. Each year closer to nine, the increase is less noticeable.

If a school district needs to curtail a music teacher's schedule, the kindergarten is usually the first to be cut. This is obviously the worst possible year to withhold music. It would be better to scale down a junior or senior high school music program. In the upper grades, a teacher can teach more music literature or present more information about music, but in kindergarten the teacher can change the children's music intelligence for life.[7]

An additional comparative study involving audiation testing and general intelligence showed a zero correlation between Stanford-Binet IQ scores and music aptitude scores.[8] One should not assume that musical potential is based on general intelligence. The commonly believed notion that mathematical abilities and music abilities are related depends on how one defines music abilities. Logical-mathematical intelligence may be related to a theoretical understanding of music, but audiation appears to be a separate intelligence from mathematics or verbal thinking. In another study, a low correlation was found between the music aptitude of parents and children.[9] It seems that the musical intelligence of children born to a family where parents provide musical experiences will be nurtured, but there is no guarantee that musical parents will pass on musical intelligence to their offspring. There were as many high-scoring children with low-scoring parents as low-scoring children with high-scoring parents. There were musical parents with

musical children and nonmusical parents with nonmusical children. These results suggest that it is not possible to base a prediction of a child's musical talent on the parents' musical aptitude.

Aptitude Versus Achievement

Children who possess high musical aptitude may not be able to reach their full musical potential. According to Gordon, music achievement will depend on a number of factors.[10] Students need a balanced diet of music experience. This includes experiences with major, minor, and other tonalities and rhythm in duple and triple as well as other meters. A broader range of experiences will enable children to assimilate a more complete understanding of musical organization.

We learn better about what something is by learning about what it is not. Formal study of meters and tonalities is not needed at this stage. It is, however, important that young children sing and move to them informally, much the way they do with language during the first five years of life. As with language, children should not be deprived of the whole musical picture because they are too young to understand it. Children learn and understand a great deal more than they can speak about during their first years, but we would never think of not speaking to infants and toddlers just because they cannot speak. The child will naturally assimilate the sophistication of the language, the grammar, and the dialect in a specific environment. When children begin to speak, they will attempt to reproduce those sounds or words that their lips and tongue can reproduce. Their comprehension of language far exceeds their ability to coordinate speech.

Music deserves the same natural assimilation. The broader the repertory and the more sophisticated the musical vocabulary, the richer will be the child's intuitive understanding of how music is organized. Children's early attempts at singing or moving to music may show a lack of coordination, but they should not be deprived of experiences that nurture comprehension before they are able to coordinate their activities.

Partners in Artistry

Attention to singing development and rhythmic moving is fundamental to the development of music aptitude. Still, music is more than tones and rhythms. It is spirit. No musical performance could be considered successful if only the tone and rhythms were present—those tones and rhythms must be performed with a deeply felt message. The ability to perform tones and rhythms with spirit is the direct outcome of music making at any age. Children would never have developed a repertory of traditional songs and rhythm solely for their tonal and rhythmic pleasure. The spirit, the joy, and the magic embodied in these songs make them appealing.

When nurturing a child's musical development, adults should ensure the selection of songs and text that are inspired, that embody a marriage of melody and spirit. Adults should select songs and rhymes that suggest childhood fantasies and are based on make-believe concepts. Imagining toes as piggies, or a knee bounce as a horse ride, will do more to inspire the musical spirit of a child than a "teaching song" that derives its inspiration from a need to educate about numbers, letters, or colors. This is not to say that teaching songs should be excluded from an early childhood curriculum, but parents and teachers should not consider their child's musical spirit nurtured through those songs. Use teaching songs to teach concepts, but use inspired repertory to enhance a child's artistry. When striving to integrate music into the preschool child's life, remember that spirit and ability are partners in artistry.

Making a Difference

If we teach to enhance all of a child's intelligences, we must include the child's music intelli-

gence. Ideally, that teaching should be provided by musically competent individuals. Regardless of musical ability, however, the best and most natural music enrichment should come from the parents. Parents should acquire collections of children's songs (or recordings if they do not read music) and memorize songs and rhymes so that children feel they are sharing a pleasurable experience with their parents rather than being made to learn a song or rhyme. Many collections of children's folk songs and rhymes are housed in the children's section of the library. Libraries also frequently present children's music programs with sing-alongs and movement activities. These are good sources from which to acquire a new song to share, but they should not be considered a substitute for the integration of music and movement into the daily routine.

Day-care and preschool teachers should plan regular music sessions. In these situations, it will be more difficult to provide the one-to-one adult-to-child interaction suited to many of the songs and rhymes, although there is the advantage of a group situation in which music games can be played that would not be practical at home. Still, day-care and preschool teachers should try to find opportunities for each child to share songs and rhymes in a one-on-one situation. Group singing does not give children opportunities to really hear themselves and know if they can produce musical sounds without assistance.[11] Parents and caregivers who feel insecure about their own singing abilities should use recorded music during music time, not as a substitute but as a partner. The children will be provided with a model of tonal and rhythmic accuracy from the recording and the spirit or joy of the activity from the eyes, face, and gestures of the adult.

One ideal solution for both parents and day-care and preschool teachers is attendance at organized music classes for preschool children. These classes are becoming increasingly common, and many well-trained musicians and educators are becoming interested in teaching this age-group. Unfortunately, the quality of preschool music programs is uneven. Stay away from those that profess to give a child a head start learning "about" music. Learning facts about music will do little to enhance a child's audiation ability. Find programs where the instructor has a pleasant singing voice and moves rhythmically in a comfortable manner. The instructor should express a real love for songs and rhymes in a playful manner and be able to evoke spiritful singing and movement responses from children of this age.

What to Expect in the Future

Everyone is talking about early childhood education. The arts community is no exception. Several state departments of education are advocating public preschool. The Connecticut Department of Education, in an effort to address the need for improved early childhood education, has extended the certification of music teachers down through nursery school. This action reflects the department's desire for colleges and universities to prepare teachers to teach this young group. Publishing companies are offering more collections of songs and rhymes for preschoolers. There is a new wave of recording artists in the hot new market of children's recording. Performances of musical artists who focus on the preschooler—artists such as Raffi and Sharon, Lois, and Bram—are consistently sold out. Even textbook publishers are investigating music curricula for the preschool years.

Future efforts may include high school classes on parenting that incorporate the arts, or videotapes to be viewed in the hospital after delivery that show mothers how to share a lullaby or other music play with their newborn. Certainly music and the other arts should be required in any early childhood college curriculum. Some colleges are already beginning to anticipate the rising need for preschool arts specialists; others seem to be waiting for state departments of education to mandate changes. Continued advocacy

and research are beginning to make a difference. Administrators are beginning to see that music and the other arts can make a difference for young children.

Caring about the whole child means caring about arts education. With the shift toward more day care, now, more than ever, parents need time and experiences to nourish their children's spirits. Music activities in the first five years are a natural means of fostering a wide variety of developmental skills. Now is the time for administrators and policymakers to recognize the many benefits the arts can offer and to understand that the arts are not as important in preschool as at other times in life. They are more important.

Notes

1. G. Alpern, T. Boll, and M. Shearer, *Developmental Profile II* (Los Angeles: Western Psychological Services, 1984).
2. K. Goodman, *What's Whole in Whole Language* (Fort Smith: Heinemann Educational Books, 1989).
3. E. D. Hirsch, *Cultural Literacy: What Every American Needs to Know* (Boston: Houghton Mifflin, 1987). See also E. D. Hirsch, *The First Dictionary of Cultural Literacy* (Boston: Houghton Mifflin, 1989).
4. H. Gardner, *Frames of Mind* (New York: Basic Books, 1983).
5. E. Gordon, *Musical Aptitude Profile* (Boston: Houghton Mifflin, 1965).
6. E. Gordon, *Primary Measures of Music Audiation* (Chicago: G.I.A., 1979).
7. Teachers and administrators who would like to investigate Gordon's research on music aptitude further should refer to his book *The Nature, Description, Measurement, and Evaluation of Music Aptitude* (Chicago: G.I.A., 1987).
8. Gordon, *The Nature.*
9. Gordon, *The Nature.*
10. E. Gordon, *Learning Sequences in Music* (Chicago: G.I.A., 1989).
11. M. Goetze, *Factors Affecting Accuracy in Children's Singing* (Ann Arbor: University Microfilms, 1985).

John Feierabend is associate professor of music education at the Hartt School of Music, University of Hartford, and coordinator of the Connecticut Center for Early Childhood Education in Music and Movement.

When constructing a developmental approach to music education, one needs to investigate the very beginnings of music making. Early childhood music educators have been most interested in Howard Gardner's writings about the acquisition of early singing competence. He reports on the search for a basic human melody or chant called the Ur-song and his quest for an answer to the question, If the Ur-song does indeed exist, how then do we go from such a song to the vast array of tunes used by each culture? He suggests that initial observations as to children's melodic and intonational babbling as well as their phonological experimentation indicate it may be inappropriate to isolate early language from early musical chanting. Gardner's presentation proposes a developmental sequence to song mastery that enables the music educator to be more accepting of the child's early song-making efforts, to anticipate appropriate responses, and plan developmentally appropriate song-making experiences for very young children.

Do Babies Sing a Universal Song?

❖

BY HOWARD GARDNER

or a long time scholars have wondered about the original language of the Bible. Was it Hebrew, another Semitic language, or some other yet-unidentified tongue? Many linguists and philologists of a less theological bent have searched for an Ur-language, a basic or original pre-Babel tongue they believe was spoken by all people in the ancient world. (*Ur* is a German prefix meaning original, primeval.)

A parallel quest has occurred in the search for a so-called Ur-song, a basic human melody or chant that nineteenth-century scholars thought was uttered by babies and believed that hunters, fishermen, and Volga boatmen continued to sing. If such a song exists, what is the nature of the melody? Where does it come from? And how do we go from the Ur-song to the vast variety of tunes and larger musical entities that are now sung or played throughout the world?

Since music seems much less tied to the events and objects of a specific culture than language is,

we may have a better chance of finding a single Ur-song than a single Ur-language. In his Charles Eliot Norton lectures at Harvard in 1973, the composer and conductor Leonard Bernstein asserted that there is a basic melody that children all over the world first chant. He even identified this Ur-song as describing an archetypal pattern of intervals on a scale. The song, Bernstein said, consists of a repetitive, descending minor third, often elaborated by an additional step of a fourth.[1] An example of a simple, repetitive, descending third would be the allegedly universal call *San*-dy, *Thom*-as. An example of the descending third with the additional fourth would be the familiar taunt "*lit*-tle *Sal*-ly *Wa*-ter" or "*al*-lee, *al*-lee *in* free!"

Taking his cue from Noam Chomsky, Bernstein claimed that the Ur-song is a joint product of our human genetic predisposition and the physical laws that govern musical harmony. As he put it, with typical flair: "These three universal notes [that is G, E, and A] are handed to us by nature on a silver platter."

Howard Gardner, "*Do Babies Sing a Universal Song?" Psychology Today* (December 1981). Reprinted with permission from *Psychology Today* magazine. Copyright © 1981 (Sussex Publishers, Inc.).

Other scholars, for example the noted ethnomusicologist Bruno Nettl, express some sympathy for the notion of a set of basic chants from which the world's diverse melodies are spawned. But in a time of cultural relativism, Bernstein's belief that the harmonic system favored by the West has furnished a universal Ur-song has been challenged by many observers. A less ethnocentric consensus claims that even the initial songs of children reflect the predominant melodic, harmonic, and rhythmic practices of their culture. Children are not raised in an acoustic vacuum. The tunes they sing no less than the words they repeat will reflect the sounds they hear in their society rather than some universal, preordained pattern.

In truth, however, little has been established about the early development of singing. Ultimately, only careful studies of children all over the world can establish the validity of the Ur-song proposal. In the meantime, however, we can get some intriguing cues about human song by studying the creatures to whom singing seems to come most naturally: the birds.

Studying Birdsong

A survey of birdsong reveals a phenomenon of bewildering variety. Some species have one song; others, more than a thousand. Some species exhibit great individual differences among "singers"; others show only minute variations. Some species learn songs throughout life; others seem capable of learning only during the first year. But is there an avian Ur-song?

It is possible to conduct experiments with birds, raising them in isolation or even deafening them, to see what will happen to their songs. One can even experiment with areas of the bird brain involved in song production and observe the effects on the usual patterns of development.

Such studies have been done over the past few decades by several imaginative investigators, including Fernando Nottebohm, W. H. Thorpe, and Peter Marler. Their findings, of enormous complexity, are constantly being revised and refined. Yet Nottebohm discerns three major patterns in the development of birdsong.

In some species, for example the ringdove, there apparently is a single song that is eventually produced by every male member of the species. Here in nature is our Ur-song. Yet the ringdove needs no auditory feedback (hearing its own song) or external stimulation (hearing other ringdoves singing). Essentially, the fledgling will produce the same song even if isolated—and deafened—during the so-called critical period when the birdsong is typically learned.

For most birds, however, song development is more complex. Typically, birds begin with a period of sub-song—a rambling, low-amplitude kind of vocalization that apparently serves no communicative purpose and lasts but a few weeks. This "babble" is followed for a somewhat longer period by plastic song, a lengthier sound segment with syllables that constitute short phrases. The syllables and phrases are delivered variably for several months. Finally, usually within a year, the "drill" of plastic song gives way to a stereotyped song or songs that will be similar to those produced by all adult males of the species.

Against this background of normal song development, scientists can examine the effect of various deprivations. Canaries represent one instructive pattern: They require auditory feedback for normal development, but they can go it alone. They prove able to produce a well-structured song even without hearing others in their species vocalize. However, if they are deafened before the period of vocal learning, they will produce a song that is highly abnormal. It is more crucial for them to hear themselves than to monitor other members of the species.

A third pattern, at the opposite extreme from the ringdove's, is exemplified by the chaffinch, a bird much studied in England. The chaffinch needs both auditory feedback *and* exposure to other chaffinches if it is to produce a full, normal song. If deafened within the first three months of life, the chaffinch will produce an extremely abnormal song, one that may be little more than a continuous screech. However, if an adult is deafened after learning its song, there is no deterioration in performance.

The Biology of Birdsong

Researchers are beginning to understand some of the biological roots of birdsong. For example, birdsong turns out to be one of the very few instances of brain lateralization in the entire animal kingdom. Just as the brain's left hemisphere is critical for language production and language comprehension in human beings, so the left hypoglossal nerve in the bird proves crucial for its song production. We also know that the production or the suppression of the hormone testosterone in both male and female birds is highly connected to song production. Given sufficient testosterone, the female, who usually does not sing, will be able to master the repertoire of songs in the same way as the male.

Thus even in the apparently simple organism of the bird there is really no single, approved course for the development of song. The ringdoves provide comfort for those in search of an Ur-song, while the canaries and chaffinches exhibit a pattern closer to the one proposed by cultural relativists. Nevertheless, the basic sequence—a babbling subsong followed by a more flexible plastic song with a large number of bits, all of which are finally pruned into a more stereotyped song at about the time of maturity—serves as a highly suggestive model for the development of human musical skills.

But perhaps it is more pertinent to compare the development of musical skills in human beings with the growth of other symbol systems.

Discovering Symbol Systems

In the case of language, an initial period of babbling is found among all children, even those who are deaf or blind. Children utter sounds common to all languages early in their first year, but increasingly produce only sounds heard in their cultural milieu. Following a period of relative quiet, they go on to produce their first meaningful words of communication—"doggie," "cookie," "mine." By the age of two, they are stringing together two or three words in meaningful utterances. By the age of three, they can produce sentences of some complexity. Syntactic ability flowers in the third and fourth years of life, giving rise to a great variety of grammatical structures as well as considerable expressive power. And by the age of four or five, most children are able to produce simple stories of some originality and considerable spirit.

In the development of drawing, we find a similar pattern. In their second year, children begin to make marks on pieces of paper and seem to enjoy it. At first, the scribbles are apparently unorganized, though they tend to reflect circular and jabbing motor activities that are readily carried out with a pencil grasped in the hand. In the third year, children are able to produce a variety of geometric forms, such as squares, circles, crosses, and mandalas: they seem to be trying to master different shapes rather than representing objects.

A dramatic watershed occurs around the age of three or four, when children become able to combine geometric forms into coherent and recognizable shapes and to associate them deliberately with objects in the world. We then encounter tadpole figures of human beings as well as simple graphic representations of dogs, horses, tables, houses, birds, suns, and the other staples of childhood art everywhere. By the age of five or six, children can produce organized compositions of some complexity and interest; observers of children's painting speak of a flowering of artistic activity in that period.[2]

As part of a more comprehensive study of the development of competence across diverse symbolic domains, my colleagues Lyle Davidson, Patricia McKernon, and Dennie Wolf at Harvard's Project Zero have been observing the development of musical abilities in a group of nine children during the first five years of life. This study has provided a fine-grained appreciation of the steps involved in early musical mastery of a group of first-born youngsters in a Western middle-class milieu. It does not solve the riddle of the Ur-song, but it suggests some of the dimensions of the acquisition of early singing competence.

Initial observations confirm that children's babbling includes melodic and intonational as well as phonological experimentation. Indeed, it may be inappropriate to isolate early language from early musical chanting; the two appear to be indissolubly linked.

Imitation, Pitch Matching, and Song Mastery

Nonetheless, two events of potential musical significance stand out during the first year of life. First, children prove capable of imitating the intonational patterns of linguistic structures they hear around them. Indeed, imitation of the "song qualities" of speech and singing seems more prominent during the first year than imitation of more focused aspects of communication. Second, many children seem able to match specific pitches with far greater than chance accuracy. According to William Kessen and Janice Levine, if an experimenter sings particular pitches, an infant will sing them back with some accuracy. While there may not be a direct link from intonational and pitch matching to ultimate singing mastery, no doubt such "computational" capacities reflect the kinds of basic skills on which musical achievement will eventually be constructed.

What about the specific steps in mastery of song beyond the first year of life? The passage is long and complex, but it is worth indicating at least some of the highlights.

The first melodic fragments produced by children at about one year or fifteen months have no strong musical identity. Their undulating patterns, going up and down over a very brief interval, are more reminiscent of waves than of particular pitch attacks. Indeed, a quantum leap occurs at about the age of a year and a half, when for the first time children can intentionally produce discrete pitches. It is as if diffuse babbling has now been supplanted by specific punctuated words.

The course for the next year is quite regular. The first intervals sung by children tend to be seconds, minor thirds, and major thirds. In the second and third years, children embark on a seemingly systematic drill of each of those intervals as they appear in fragments; they also engage in a process of continuing expansion of the intervals, from the tiny seconds and thirds noted by Bernstein and Nettl to larger intervals, including fourths and fifths.

We may speak at this time of spontaneous song, the production of numerous fragments consisting of seconds, thirds, and occasionally fourths. Like the early subsong of the bird, however, these patterns are undefined and unmemorable. They appear to lack organization, having little of our adult sense of tonality or harmony, and are rhythmically irregular; jotting them down accurately poses a notational challenge even for the musically trained ear.

By the age of two or two and a half, a new phenomenon emerges. For the first time, children exhibit explicit awareness of the tunes sung by others in their environment. Familiar nursery rhymes—"A-B-C-D," "Old MacDonald," "Happy Birthday," "Twinkle, Twinkle, Little Star"— now stand out for the children as well. They make fledgling efforts to reproduce these songs; thus we need to introduce a contrast here between spontaneous song and learned song.

In the beginning, children's efforts at learned song are little more than melodic fragments they have been producing in spontaneous song. The only way we can confirm that a child is actually attempting to produce a song from the culture is in the production of some telltale lyric, such as "H-I-J-K-LMNOP" or "an oink-oink here, an oink-oink there." The lyrics and the spontaneous song carry the day.

Toward the end of the third year, however, the spontaneous song begins to become uncoupled from the learned song. That occurs because the child has acquired a sense of the rhythmic structure of the song; thus efforts at learned song bear not only a lyrical, but also a rhythmic resemblance to the learned cultural model.

It would be misleading to suggest that by this age, a child already knows the songs of the culture or even that he or she has a developed frame for a particular song. Rather, the child knows characteristic bits or embryonic tune segments that can be repeated over and over again. Here again, one is reminded of birdsong, particularly the period of phrase song. This is a time when the child is apparently working with the building blocks of song: exploring small segments, practicing them, combining them in diverse ways so that they bear a kind of family resemblance to the target song but do not yet reveal its general structure. One is reminded of an orchestra as it tunes up for a performance, a time when a keen ear can pick out the important fragments but not the shape of the piece to be performed.

A sea change occurs at about the age of three or four. For the first time, the child goes beyond the characteristic bits of a phrase and attempts to reproduce the overall learned song heard from the larynxes (and phonographs) in the environment. Now the learned song comes to dominate the spontaneous song, rather than the reverse. Further, the learned song exhibits those regular intervals and rhythms that remain difficult to discern in the simpler and less organized spontaneous songs. In fact, the child has a sense of the overall structure of the song and can even subordinate particular parts of the song to the overall song structure. Nonetheless, at this age the child still relies mostly on lyrics and rhythm to make the songs recognizable to others. Lacking a well-developed sense of key and tonality, the child is generally restricted to the overall contour of the song, its ups and downs, and to an approximate sense of tonal values.

Learning a New Song

Since it is difficult to study just how children arrive at song mastery in their natural environment, we have found it helpful in our studies to teach them a song they have not heard before and to observe the steps they go through in learning it. Lyle Davidson and Patricia McKernon taught our four-and five-year-old subjects an old folk tune called "The Charlie Song." This deceptively simple melody resembles those that children readily acquire at this age but has sufficient melodic, rhythmic, and lyrical complexity to reveal the kinds of problems they encounter (and the strategies they use) in proceeding from a skeletal to a fleshed-out version of a song.

Happily, our children were able to learn "The Charlie Song." But they didn't learn it right away. By their initial failures as well as their early successes, they helped to clarify some of the later aspects of song mastery.

Our four-year-olds readily learn the words to the song. Indeed, one might say that the meaning of the song first inheres in its words. Shortly afterward, the children are able to acquire the surface rhythm of the song, which of course is closely yoked to the actual linguistic phrases.

The next major step involves mastering the contour of the song. The child at age four, or a little bit thereafter, has a sense of when a song goes up, when it goes down, and the approximate size of the leaps in either direction. What is lacking is an accurate sense of interval mapping (the ability to produce a fourth versus a fifth reliably) and a key sense that remains stable across phrases (for example, remaining in the key of C rather than shifting to the key of D or G). The child may well remain within the same key during a short phrase and be able to reproduce a large leap. But the precision needed for accurate song rendition is not yet available.

In the other symbol systems, we find the same trend between the ages of three and five. At the beginning of this period, children exhibit a kind of approximate or "topological" mapping that enables them to capture general size and spatial relationships. For example, in drawing a person, they will get the relation between body parts or the number of toes and fingers approximately, but not exactly, correct. Toward the end of this age span, children exhibit digital or numerical mapping, which permits them to master and retain specific distances, proportions, and numbers. This kind of progress is clear in song development during the fourth and fifth years.

By the end of the fifth year, following considerable practice with "The Charlie Song," the average child has reached two milestones. The first

lar, repeated pulse, a metronomic beat that organizes the way the various rhythmic structures should be articulated. To put it pragmatically, the child can now beat time at regular intervals throughout the song rather than simply being carried along by the stress patterns of the particular syllables.

The second, possibly more complex acquisition, involves mastery of the tonal elements of "The Charlie Song." The child advances a long way toward the digital precision described above. On the one hand, he or she has attained sufficient mastery to produce particular intervals with increasing precision: a third is a third, a fifth is a fifth, and they can be heard as such even by someone unfamiliar with the tonal intervals of the song. On the other hand, of equal importance, the child now acquires the knowledge (and the appreciation) that there is a single organizing key that pervades the entire song. If the song is in the key of C, that means that it should begin in C, remain in C in the absence of an explicit modulation to another key, and, in general, close at the end in the tonic of C. That task is largely accomplished in most normal children by the age of five.

involves the ability to extract the underlying pulse from the surface rhythm. Initially, the child's sensitivity to rhythm derives strictly from the placement of accents in the surface lyrics; ultimately, the child comes to appreciate that, underlying these surface rhythms, there is a regu-

How close is the typical five-year-old to adult competence in song? Some intriguing clues can be obtained from a recent study by Davidson, who asked beginning vocal students at the New England Conservatory of Music to learn our "Charlie Song." These gifted young adults naturally displayed less difficulty in learning the song, and some in fact exhibited "one-trial learning." But they also made many of the same errors the children did. For example, both groups regularized the rather unusual A-B-A-C plan of the song to a more canonical A-B-A-B form. The adults also made the same kinds of pitch mistakes as the children—intervals of seconds were inappropriately transformed to the more predictable intervals of thirds or fifths.

Perhaps the principal difference between the younger and older groups was that the adults already knew numerous folk songs of the "Charlie" variety. Accordingly, they tried to fit the new tune into song structures, or schemas, that they had already mastered—sometimes to their advantage, sometimes not. In contrast, the young children were still in the process of forming initial schemas. And so they were less likely to distort "The Charlie Song" to fit into the pre-established mold of, say, "This Old Man" or "Greensleeves."

Whether it be music, language, or drawing, the child begins in infancy with a period of free exploration, using elements devoid of significance, such as individual tones, phonemic bundles, or discrete line. That is followed by a somewhat longer period in which the child explores somewhat larger units, or building blocks, such as words, geometric forms, or melodic bits. Only in the third or fourth year of life does the child come to combine these building blocks into culturally approved products, like learned songs, simple stories, or representational drawings.

It is at this point in development that the forms favored by the culture exert increasing influence over, and eventually dominate, the characteristic bits that the children have been producing on their own with relatively little instruction. Thus we might say that any impulses toward the development of a universal Ur-song, Ur-story, or Ur-sketch are permanently squelched at this time. Indeed, children seem predisposed at a certain point in development to acquire the forms of the culture:

in the absence of cultural instruction, it seems likely that development would cease altogether.

Musical development is scarcely completed at age five. Though five-year-olds can sing a good tune, only exceptional youngsters will play instruments, use musical notation, or appreciate the various interpretations available for a given song or score. Five-year-olds lack knowledge of music and music theory. And it may well be that the way they think about music, or the way that they think musically, continues to change as they grow older. About these matters we know very little.

As one who studied piano for many years in childhood and who continues to draw emotional sustenance from music, I know that early encouragement of musical skills can be important. Yet I also believe that for many children, the start of formal musical instruction marks the beginning of the end of musical development. The atomistic focus in most musical instruction—the individual pitch, its name, its notation—and the measure-by-measure method of instruction and analysis run counter to the holistic way most children have come to think of, react to, and live with music. (In contrast, a notation that simply marks where the piece becomes louder or softer, higher or lower, might be readily assimilated by young children.) Often the clash of these world views proves too jarring, and the child's musical flair becomes dimmer or even withers away. In fact, the challenge of musical education is to respect and build upon the young child's own skills and understanding of music rather than to impose a curriculum designed largely for adults.

Notes

1. An example of a third would be the interval between "this" and "old" in the tune that begins "This old man." A fourth would be the interval between "Don" and "ald" in "Old MacDonald had a farm."
2. See "Children's Art: The Age of Creativity," *Psychology Today* (May 1980).

Howard Gardner, a research psychologist, is codirector of Harvard's Project Zero, a research group that studies artistic thinking.

Understanding the spontaneous musical behaviors of children is essential if we are to involve ourselves in an effective child-centered approach to learning. In the late thirties, The Pillsbury Foundation School engaged in an in-depth study of "how creative music activity was provoked and generated in young children, and to explore how the teacher should provide technical assistance and information when the opportunity arose." The findings of this longitudinal study have had far-reaching effects on current early childhood music learning environments and the ability to predict children's musical behaviors. Donald Pond, the school's first music director, reflected on his experiences in an article for the *Music Educators Journal*. These early findings continue to be applicable in that they confirmed the importance of free exploratory play and hands-on learning materials. His statement to educators is timeless: "It is up to us as teachers to nurture rather than repress the deeply rooted natural musicality that young children inherit and to use our intelligence and creative imagination to foster its healthy growth from those roots."

The Young Child's Playful World of Sound

BY DONALD POND

"Our differentiated consciousness is in continual danger of being uprooted; hence it needs compensation through the still existing state of childhood."

—Carl Jung, in
Essays on a Science of Mythology

n 1936, attorney Evan S. Pillsbury left a legacy to establish a foundation for the advancement of music education. To determine how the funds might be most usefully spent, the three appointed trustees sought the advice of conductor Leopold Stokowski. He told them that what he thought was most needed was an in-depth study of the spontaneous music and musicality of young children, and he suggested that they establish a school for this purpose. Stokowski, who was acquainted with my work at the Dalton School in New York City, attended by one of his daughters, recommended me for the position of the school's music

director. I held that position from January 1937 to the end of December 1944.

Between fifteen and twenty, three- to six-year-old children were enrolled in the Pillsbury Foundation School randomly. No priority was given to musically gifted students. My responsibility was to observe the spontaneous creativity of unindoctrinated normality, not the budding of specialized genius. I was fortunate to have access to an extensive musical instrument collection, and I selected several appropriate instruments for the children to use—marimbas (including a Balinese *saron*), gongs, bells, drums, cymbals, and rattles. I added other instruments from time to time as the need became apparent. The children were allowed to use these instruments in any part of the room, on the porch, or in the yard, and none of the instruments ever was damaged. A small, curtained stage was constructed, and it often was used in creative activity. The children also could operate a phonograph without having to ask permission. I tried to make careful and appropriate choices of the

Donald Pond, "The Young Child's Playful World of Sound," *Music Educators Journal* 66, no. 7 (March 1980): 38–41.

recordings, which improved as I continued to observe the children and analyze their needs.

Within the environment of the Pillsbury School, freedom was provided for the children to ride on tricycles and in wagons, to run and dance, to play instruments and sing, to have parades, to give shows, to invent plays, and to celebrate spontaneously festive occasions. This freedom did not interfere with their required academic studies, guided by an able, certified teacher. One of my functions was to try to discover how creative music activity was provoked and generated in young children, and to give technical assistance and information when the opportunity arose. I was always ready, when invited, to join in the children's music-making. I thought of myself not so much as a teacher, but as a musician and composer whose special skills and knowledge were always available but never imposed on the students, and whose sensitivities permitted me to hear and see what they were doing, to understand its significance, and to keep accurate records. After almost eight years of day-to-day creative companionship with young children, I collected enough material to come to some conclusions about the emergence of their musicality and the roots from which it sprang.

To uncover those roots was the objective I set for myself when I began to explore the young child's world of music, without knowing, however, that young children, in their relationship to music, already were being systematically redirected by the ignorantly unexamined methodologies of the music education establishment. Deeply rooted awareness of auditory phenomena is primary, and it is the young child's innate possession from the first moment of his or her existence. Surely nothing can be more basic to emerging musicality. First a child becomes aware of sounds, then he or she experiences wonder and delight, and then an insatiable exploration begins of sonorities as wide as the environment can provide. This process has nothing to do with music as we commonly know it, but everything to do with music as it actually exists—nakedly primeval at the roots. But unless we have been privileged to share, to experience vicariously, what young children perceive, we can in no way apprehend that music.

First Musical Encounters

In the beginning of a child's encounters with music is sound—but out of the chaos can emerge a created sound-shape. I discovered that without the chaos no creation can be possible.

I also observed the children's primary impulse to set sounds in motion—not to invent rhythm patterns, which developed shortly thereafter, but to compel a sequence of sound impulses into wave-like movement by means of accentuation. This impulse reflected in part muscular stresses and relaxations, but I also believe that the rhythmic irregularity occurred as the result of the students' will, and that invention for the sake of delight was taking place. It seemed to me that the children's indefinite potential for discovering rhythmic articulation was a continual source of pleasure for them.

This delight was evident not only in their use of instrumental sounds, but also in the way they made accent patterns with their voices. We can see in the young child's emergent musicality that there are exposed predilections that relate intimately to the structural freedom of musical rhythm, which is often neglected, perhaps because it has nothing to do with "learning to count."

Rhythmically, everything was rooted in that wave-like movement of sound impulses created by spontaneous accentuations. Subsequently, beat subdivision made possible the invention of more complex rhythmic figures and rhythm patterns, but the basis, with its accented irregularity, still was there. Please note that I have said nothing about meter because I regard it as artificial and not deeply rooted. When meter did develop later, it tended to be the product of auxiliary circumstances such as dancing or other patterned movement, or of metrically disposed verbal arrangements.

To describe what I discovered about vocal melody, I should begin by recounting what I did not discover. "Melody" is a word that too often is stereotypically perceived and defined. The children's melodies were not based on or even suggestive of classical harmonies or scales. The melodies did not progress or end predictably. Nor did they conform to preexistent metric contrivances.

Song and Chant

I named the children's two types of vocal melodies "song" and "chant." The songs were personal, unpremeditated, and evanescent, which made them extremely difficult to capture. The words, when used, tended to be imaginative, descriptive, anecdotal, lyrical, or nonsensical. Song melodies were capricious but moved within a narrow range that rarely exceeded a sixth and used intervals no longer than a third. Characteristically the movement was regular, with one note to a syllable, the accentuation was verbally rather than arbitrarily determined, and the rhythms moved freely; however, syllables could be lengthened to contain clusters of two or more notes, and sometimes exuberant melismas resulted. In general the melodies of these tiny songs seemed to represent a young child's enjoyment of intervals themselves, and abrupt, leaping changes of tessitura were common and apparently pleasurable.

The two-note chant melody was based on a descending minor third. This interval is an omnipresent, immeasurably ancient, and socially oriented vocal structure. And again, it is deeply rooted in the world of the young child. A chant usually was initiated by one child, but it was directed to the entire group. After the singing of a chant had begun, other children soon joined in, either in imitation or, more often, by inventing individual verbal and rhythmic variations. Impromptu singing games that used chants were a favorite form of spontaneous, communal music-making at the school. Even the three-year-old children were able to enjoy them. Musical inventiveness in such a diverse group was possible only because the children had been encouraged to be musical and creative, close to the roots of their own being, without inhibition.

The chant melody pitches were later extended by an ascending perfect fourth (for example G-E-A-G-E), and simultaneously a characteristic rhythm pattern of long-short-short long-long was created. The only added note I ever heard in either form of the chant melody was a minor second, F, above the lowest note, E; so that instead of being identified as pentatonic, the melody could be construed as being contained within a Phrygian tetrachord. Be that as it may, the dominating and deeply rooted presence of the minor third in the young child's musical world was clearly evident.

I also observed an innate predilection for shaping sounds into structural forms, particularly through imitation and variation. The spontaneous singing of embryonic canons seemed especially to delight the young students.

The children played with sounds uninhibitedly, but not at random; the games they played were concerned, however tentatively or primitively, with the structuring of sounds. I believe that if we are to arrive at an objective understanding of the young child's emergent musicality, these observations must be regarded as pivotal. What seems to me to be a major and destructive misconception is the notion that musical creativity in early childhood originates from a compulsion for self-expression. The compulsion that I observed was for being a maker, an inventor of sound shapes, and for creating linear movement and enjoying the patterns that simultaneously moving lines of sounds could produce. Additionally, the children exhibited an instinctive and ingenious faculty for devising and sustaining spontaneous polyrhythms of sometimes baffling complexity and for enjoying their seemingly effortless repetition.

Polyphonic improvisation thus should be viewed as a fundamental element of early childhood music experiences—whether it be the antiphonal or canonic singing of chants or the heterophonic playing of instruments. It is through improvisation that music grows naturally from its roots in the young child—free; having no relationship to anything that their teachers learn in theory classes; and subject to no arbitrary laws of scale construction, or harmony, or of form.

I noticed that any aspect of the young child's discovery of sound (apart from solo song) did not remain a private, self-oriented activity. Everything that could be useful to the whole class was absorbed speedily into their everyday lives and instantly became community property. But they displayed no strutting or superior attitudes, because the concept of the "artist" had no place at the roots. The unaffected spontaneity of the children's music-making invited participation from all who would collaborate actively or would form an audience. The children's dramatic play rarely lacked appropriately integrated music improvisations. And all occasions for celebration and ritual observance provoked musical invention.

It is up to us as teachers to nurture rather than repress the deeply rooted natural musicality that young children inherit and to use our intelligence and creative imagination to foster its healthy growth from those roots. If we do this with humility and dedication, children will grow up in their own world of sound to make inventions that will belong to them and their community and that will be integrated into its social life for the sake of celebration and delight.

A young child is able to savor a single sound as a unique experience. He or she can enjoy the god-like ability to make an inert, inarticulate object produce sound. All music, all delight in music, all authentic acts of musical invention are rooted in this seminal musicality—a music appreciation such as no method can circumscribe nor any classroom instruction impart. Here we are irreducibly at the roots, and we had better see to it that what we have learned by rote we do not use to frustrate our children's unarguable instincts and so alienate them from their own musical beings.

Donald Pond, a composer and music educator who died in 1983, served as music director of the Pillsbury Foundation from 1937 to 1944. Pond's papers, including his writings and compositions, are available through the MENC Historical Center. For further information, see Judith Kerschner Kierstead, "The Pillsbury Foundation School and Beyond," Master's thesis. University of Maryland at College Park, 1991.

When interacting musically with young children, allowing for freedom of choice, experimentation, individual time on task, and the right to work at one's own developmental level is a major concern. This freedom cannot be achieved when the sole approach to the music experience is in a large-group music-making setting. Throughout this book, each author alludes to or strongly advocates the importance of exploratory, spontaneous, creative play in setting a developmentally appropriate learning environment. In developing such an environment, the teacher must often create areas in which individual or small-group music play can occur. The settings must contain objects and music-motivating material that can be heard and manipulated. Such items inherently lead to musical awareness, understanding, performance, and other interactions with sound. The early childhood music teacher becomes responsible for creating, assembling, and purchasing materials that are especially designed to arouse the child's curiosity and disposition towards music.

In the seventies, music educators were just becoming aware of the exploratory-play facet of the early childhood music program. Model materials were created and suggestions for learning environments were shared. The suggestions remain valid for today's early childhood classrooms and should provide impetus for the creation of additional musical play materials and learning areas devised or purchased by the teacher.

Music in Early Childhood

The Environment

BY BARBARA L. ANDRESS, HOPE HEIMANN,
CARROLL RINEHART, AND GENE TALBERT

The Child
I am a bit of breath
soft,
lovable.
I look out at all I see and wonder.

I cling to your hand ready to be shown,
I am fearful
I am reckless.

I know best that which I see, touch, hear, smell
...taste
What shall I see, touch, hear, smell, taste?

With what will you help me fill my life?
Where will you guide me?
How will I go?

I can continue to look and wonder
Or through understanding, I can
look
in wonder
—and marvel.

—*Barbara L. Andress*

 room filled with people and things and feelings: the environment. It is both a place and an atmosphere. A room that feels sunny, filled with the murmur of voices engaged in purposeful activity, is the beginning of an environment inviting exploration and learning experiences. There should be freedom and there should be control, with the two working together instead of at opposite poles. There should be order but not through rigid or compulsive restrictions. Children should feel comfortable knowing that this is their room to plan in, to share, and to be responsible for.

It is the teacher's responsibility to prepare this environment both in its physical aspects and the more subtle psychological manifestations. The two are intertwined and one cannot function well without the other. Beautiful equipment may remain untouched and unexplored in an overly structured atmosphere. Conversely, neither can a warm and responsive climate without fresh

Barbara L. Andress, Hope Heimann, Carroll Rinehart, and Gene Talbert, "The Environment," in *Music in Early Childhood* (Reston, VA: Music Educators National Conference, 1973). Revised 1991. This publication was originally prepared under the supervision of Barbara L. Andress for the MENC National Commission on Instruction.

new things and challenges lead to expanded frontiers of learning.

Preparing the Environment for Musical Learning

What makes up the effective learning environment? Space, light, things to explore, and freedom to explore. All this tempered by ground rules mutually understood and agreed upon so that the explorations will not lead to chaos. The teacher may prepare the environment for both specific and general encounters prior to the children's arrival. Certain objects are set up to provide the playful chance encounter in special topical (music) areas. Preparations for area play may be very simple, using sounds and equipment that are readily available, or they may be as sophisticated as funds, the readiness of the children, and the teacher's creative imagination will allow.

The teacher also must be prepared to create an environment on the spot for that *unplanned teachable moment.* While the children are busy at play, the adult is constantly alert, observing them for cues to determine their readiness for appropriate musical experiences. The teacher does not feel bound to the structured plan but is prepared to seize the moment when the child's interest abruptly changes or curiosity is piqued during random play, conversations, or investigations.

Sometimes those random investigations with things that make sounds result in noise to the teacher's ear. The adult should be ready for this aural fallout and be careful not to respond to it negatively. If appropriate, the experimentation may be guided from noise to organized sound, with the teacher guiding patiently and gently after the child has been allowed a reasonable amount of exploration. What constitutes a reasonable amount of time? One session? One week? One month? This varies from group to group,

child to child, and teacher to child. There can be no precise answer. But the child's own experimentation is essential as the first stage of learning. Without some guidance, structure, and introduction of new ideas along the way, the child may be content with "banging and rattling" instruments for an indefinite period of time. If the purpose is to help the children discover *music* as well as just discover sounds, sooner or later the teacher must enter the scene. Such intervention is not to impose ideas and concepts, but to offer them for consideration. If that which is demonstrated is valid, young children will imitatively play and attempt to make the model their own.

Exploring Instrumental and Found Sounds

Children should have an opportunity to produce sounds and become aware of the many different timbres that abound. They should become aware that such sound objects are influenced by size, shape, material, and sound starters. Such items may be found in the environment: paper, plastic, metal, wood, sandpaper, stones, or emanate from traditional musical instruments. Children may play with the sounds of water—water in the kitchen, in nature, dripping, pouring, and rushing. They may hear instruments that make loud sounds, soft sounds, or are silent at times. Games of sound and silence can help develop an awareness of the intentional, peripheral, and continual sounds of life.

Children must listen to valid musical sounds. They cannot grow in musical sensitivity unless provided with many opportunities to hear and explore music and musical instruments that are tonally accurate and produce quality musical timbres. The child may at times play with pie tins and plastic bottles filled with rice, but must also have many experiences with fine brass cymbals and wooden maracas. The child also needs to explore the more complex and fragile musical instruments. The teacher must determine how and when this may be appropriately accomplished.

The teacher must be consistent in allowing all visible objects to be touched and played. Instruments not to be used by children should be kept out of sight. These initial encounters should be planned in order to avoid any unhappy misunderstandings and damage either to the child's feelings toward discovery or to the physical structure of the instrument. It probably would be easier to repair the damage to the instrument than to the child, but it is wiser to avoid the need for either.

One way to introduce an orchestral instrument might be to guide a listening experience. Children might hear a skilled musician play the instrument, tell about it, and pass it around to be touched most respectfully. The child should have many listening experiences and exposures to many kinds of music and musical instruments.

Models of Musical Sounds

Different instruments and voices, both solo and in ensemble, live when possible but also on record or tape should be part of the music learning environment. A collection of recordings does not have to be extensive as young children are very comfortable with and look forward to repetition. The collection should include music of many styles and periods (classical, folk, and pop) performed by various musical organizations (large and small vocal and instrumental groups).

Expressing Music through Movement

Movement experiences in response to music should be available and encouraged. The environment necessary for the child's movement activity is created simply by moving things to create an open space. An open space and an open climate are the basic needs. For some experiences, even the open space area can be quite small. Good things happen for most people in the open climate. Teacher, child, space, things, curiosity, control, and patience all interweave to make a place where exciting discoveries are made and new experiences happen— a stimulating yet calm, creative environment.

Ideas for Setting the Environment

Preschool children play with and respond to musical sounds to enjoy and better understand their function. The child imitates his or her world and uses body and vocal sounds to express feelings and understandings. Musical examples are heard and imitated or otherwise expressed. It is soon discovered that the range and variety of sounds may be extended through the use of instruments: A drum can play louder than the hands can clap. The young child needs time to gain control of his or her body and to learn how to express ideas. Likewise, time is needed to explore how instruments will respond and how they can be controlled. The child explores how materials will respond, uses them for expressive purposes, and then ultimately, discovers alternative or more structured uses for the same materials.

The purpose for which one explores and utilizes music and sound becomes critical to the learning process. The teacher's clue to guiding these experiences lies in the ability to interpret behaviors as evidence of specific growth. Exploratory settings using instruments are specialized to meet the needs of the young learner. For example, the adult makes available pairs of small percussion instruments so that the game can extend beyond single sound exploration to matching and classifying challenges. The teacher will want to devise and continually search for interesting sounds or traditional instruments to arouse the child's curiosity toward musical play.

A Place to Play with Musical Sounds and Ideas

Arrangement of the room should allow for many types of activities, especially space for movement. A child may wish to improvise even when the rest of the group is involved in other activities. Maintain an open space in which this kind of experience can happen spontaneously.

Young children, at times need private space within the context of the busy preschool classroom or care center in which to explore musical sounds and ideas. Such spaces allow some control of the many other visual and auditory distractors that are rampant in an active hands-on classroom setting. Special places to explore sounds or topically focus on music-making tasks may be created by using decorated oversize cardboard boxes. For example, make a cardboard box dog house displaying the dog's name "Bingo" in which to play out the familiar song, or use several large containers such as commercial laundry soap cans (approximately three feet tall and two feet in diameter) to create music-making carrels. Cut different shaped entrance holes in the carrels and leave the lid on top. Increase the size of the carrel by combining two or more cans. Cut a large hole between the two containers on the sides where they are joined. Paint the cans bright colors. Place these carrels randomly about the room. Invite children to bring a sound with them when they enter.

A "see me, hear me, feel me" box provides a special environment for sound studies. This sound center may be as simple as a large cardboard box with one or two crawl holes through which the child can enter and interact with different sound ideas, or this box could be constructed from plywood, tri-wall, or other sturdy cardboard to become a permanent part of the room's equipment.

Make the box a four-foot cube with a removable lid so that various sound ideas can be inserted through the top of the box. Add a drop-in false wall on one side of the box for easy installation of sound exploration materials. For example, assorted size hand drums may be attached to the false wall with several different sound starters (mallets, beaters, sticks) placed on the floor of the box for child's use.

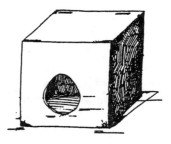

Exploration spaces may also be purchased from toy shops or construction material outlets. Items such as small tents, cardboard playhouses, and cement tube forms can be exciting places in which to enjoy music.

Often the child only needs an area marked to indicate the play space and activity. Other children are cautioned to respect this area and not interfere with the activity unless invited. Such an area might be defined by using a small rug. The child may take the rug and "sounds" to a spot of his or her own choice. Additional ways to mark play spaces are to make masking tape circles, or place a hula hoop on the floor to contain small instruments or music games such as a guitar.

Ideally, at least two audiocassette tape players should be available for use in the classroom. This allows for children's and teacher's use and for recorded music to be available in a carrel or other special play area. Try creating a "Be a Clown Dress-Up and Dance Corner." Place clown paraphernalia such as hats, collars, and yarn wigs in the designated area. Have recorded music playing on a continuous audiotape loop such as "The March" from *The Comedians* by Dmitry Kabalevsky. Children can dress up and move expressively to the music.

Planned Sound Plays

A bank of sounds and planned sound plays can be housed in a designated area of the room in individual containers. The child can then rely on certain sounds or games being readily available. The sound plays should be maintained in an orderly fashion, with children expected to return materials to the storage area intact after play. Sound plays should be organized in containers to include all the play materials required for a given setting.

Inexpensive storage receptacles include plastic bleach bottles with a section cut away to serve as storage baskets. Ice cream cartons, silverware trays, or other inexpensive plastic containers accommodate uniquely shaped equipment such as mallets and sticks. Several cup hooks under the music shelf provide accessible places to hang triangles and other small percussion instruments for the child's choice of use.

The teacher needs more than just containers or places to store instruments. Games to motivate individual and small-group music making such as singing a traditional song will need to be organized for easy use by children. The teacher could prepare a song mat pictorially depicting a path leading to a school, children, and teacher. The child sings "Mary Had A Little Lamb" while moving two game pieces (Mary and the lamb) and playing out the song story. Large, colorful tag-board envelopes can be folded and taped to contain the play mat and game pieces.

Sound Sources

Whether simple or sophisticated equipment is provided for sound exploration and musical play, the media will be only as good as the many ways in which the creative teacher envisions them to be used. The following sound sources are not intended to be an inclusive list of available instruments but rather suggestions to alert the teacher to the many common and unusual pieces of equipment that can be gathered or combined for use. These types of materials can be used in musical exploration or in typical performance settings. Children will want to interact with the instruments in the open classroom environment, carrels, or other specially designated areas.

- Two sets of diatonic resonator bells. The child visually and aurally matches pitches, orders sounds, and plays patterns and melodies. It is also desirable to have a set of chromatic resonator bells so that pitch sets like the whole tone scale can be prepared for the child's use.

- Montessori-type sound sources. Prepare opaque shaker cylinders containing beans, corn, or sand for volume studies, matching, and ordering.

- Bell sets, with no visual clue to sounds, for aural discrimination, pitch matching, ordering, and playing patterns and melodies.

- Orff-type sound sources. Xylophone family instruments with removable wood or metal bars and various timbres and ranges for playing patterns, accompaniments, and melodies.

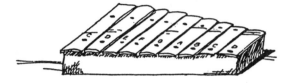

- Stairstep bells to explore melodic movement.

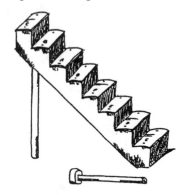

- Sounds of wood.

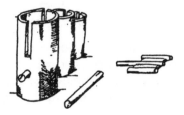

- Small percussion instruments. Be selective—look for quality sounds.

- Sound starters. The variety of sounds available from any given source will be increased by using different sound starters. The starter should never be used in such a way that the instrument is abused.

- Never refuse a gift of a string or percussion instrument! An old bass drum—what fun! What learnings? Strike a cymbal, hold it very close to the drumhead but not quite touching. What happens to the sound? How many different sound starters can be used? How will the sounds be different?

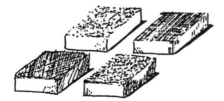

- Devised sounds—ideas that you, the teacher can construct. Different lengths of brass pipe, bamboo, wood—pitched but not tuned—suspended or cradled for playing.

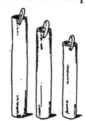

- Varying textures of sandpaper blocks for matching and ordering sounds. What would be a good sound starter?

- A little music box for a child to carry around and enjoy.

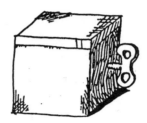

- Sounds in paper bags with different rattling objects inside. These are consumable, so the teacher or children should be prepared to remake them often.

- Kitchen implements. How are they alike? How are they different? How can the sounds be used to help tell a story?

- Commercially prepared, preschool-music sound plays, recordings, and song collections are available through various music industry outlets including MMB Music, Rhythm Band Inc., and The World of Peripole. These materials are often designed to meet the developmental needs of very young children. Many provide quality instrumental sounds and game-like approaches to exploring musical ideas. The teacher may wish to review these materials for applicability to their children's needs.

Children interact with musical ideas individually and in small and large groups. The learning environment is filled with people, things, and attitudes. Music areas must contain models, equipment, and instruments of the finest quality to trigger the child's curiosity, maintain interest, and promote growth in understanding. These resources must be organized and accessible for the child's use. The teacher's greatest effort takes place *before* children enter the preschool center or classroom. The acquisition, planning, and preparation of the resources for the musical play area are a major part of the teacher's responsibility. The teacher must feel that each interactive experience has been carefully considered from the developmental aspects of the learner and that it is musically appropriate and worthy of the child's valuable time. This requires much careful planning. The effective teacher will find that when the children arrive and enter an appropriately set environment, the only thing left to do is to enjoy interacting with the children and their music-making experiences.

Barbara L. Andress is professor emeritus in the school of music at Arizona State University—Tempe. She is an author, speaker/clinician, and currently serves as a member of the MENC Task Force on Music in Early Childhood.

Hope Heimann has retired from the field of movement education and is living in Tempe, Arizona.

Carroll Rinehart is retired from the Tucson Unified Public School District in Tucson, Arizona. He is a dynamic force in the project, Opera America, a national program that involves children in creating and performing their own operatic works.

Gene Talbert is coordinator of laboratory experiences and coordinator of learning resource centers at Tennessee Technological University in Cookeville.

Through expressive movement and music experiences the teacher can model actions, guide children by describing their actions, and couple suggestions with gestures to help them better understand the music and their own responses. Movement is especially helpful in this regard because it is a nonverbal response for young children who are in the process of developing language—and language reflects emerging thought. Movement provides a nonverbal, sensing-doing link in promoting the learning process. Frances Aronoff has long been a proponent of the use of music and movement with young children. Her article in *Music Educators Journal* provided suggestions and confirmed the validity of movement as an important learning tool in all curricular areas. She addressed music-movement as it related to the young child's language development, concepts of space and time, and skills for beginning logic and reasoning. Her contributions in this area of early childhood education have had substantial impact on current techniques and methods for dealing with movement and music in the early childhood classroom.

No Age Is Too Early to Begin

Another Look at Young Children and Music-Movement

BY FRANCES WEBBER ARONOFF

usic, music everywhere, especially in the early childhood classroom, but is the real educational challenge being met? Are we laying the kind of foundation in this area that permits the achievement of lifelong growth and benefits? Are we helping children attain the kinds of concepts and the strategies for learning that will have active and functional use in later years? The challenge before us is to provide for meaningful, viable music education, and no age is too early to begin.

The first priority is to communicate our goals for music in general education to those who make decisions about curricula. We must articulate these objectives in the language of the nonmusicians with whom we work. In the past, the placing of academic subjects at the center of the curriculum was justified because these subjects helped a person deal with the world. The

arts were peripheral—for recreation or diversion—and were usually enjoyed only by an elite minority. Music educators have talked and written at length about the need for providing music learning experiences for *all* children, but our arguments have been esoteric, theoretical, or prejudiced in favor of a particular method or music value system. In most cases, our statements have not been convincing to nonprofessional musicians.

In a practical setting, the music specialist does not have enough time to spend with the children. Working as a consultant to the classroom teacher, the specialist may be able only to prescribe specific activities and set methods. Therefore, the classroom teacher needs to be deeply involved in order to bring about the long-range benefits of developing musicality in children.

Classroom teachers of young children already use music and movement activities as means of providing for self-expression, physical release after quiet work, and social interaction; they also

Frances Webber Aronoff, "No Age Is Too Early to Begin: Another Look at Young Children and Music-Movement," *Music Educators Journal* 60, no. 7 (March 1974): 18–25.

use these activities to increase vocabulary for language development, to introduce social studies concepts, and to celebrate holidays.[1] It is essential that teachers be more aware of the intellectual growth potentials in music-movement activities: they can come to realize that children can enjoy these cognitive benefits without jeopardizing their affective growth.

Music educators should be able to explain the comprehensive role that music-movement can play in the total curriculum. So-called academic subjects may teach one how to deal with the world, but to succeed with others, people must first be able to deal with themselves. How difficult it is to explain the exhilarating impact of the music experience! Perhaps we need to reexamine our own personal experiences with music, to review how music, in unique ways, has helped us deal with ourselves, to see inside ourselves, to use our own consciousness and our own imagination.

It is a universal truth that you learn best when your whole being is involved. The young child's interweaving of his or her own thinking, feeling, and doing seems to satisfy the humanistic need for inner freedom. The younger the child, the easier it is to foster this interrelationship through music-movement experiences. In effect, the child is the musical instrument—thinking, feeling, and doing in a nonthreatening setting.[2]

There has been considerable researching and theorizing about young children's learning. We have heard much about intellectual growth in the early years, conceptual learning, the redefinition of intelligence to include factors of creativity, competence as a comprehensive educational goal, and the open classroom.

Music-Movement in the Total Curriculum

1. Basic Language Skills
  a. Auditory attention and discrimination
  b. Listening comprehension
  c. Learning to communicate
  d. Language for thinking

Listen to the sound you made
Make it over and over and over
                              Listen!
Sing or make funny sounds to go with your own walking
                                        rocking
                                        seesawing
                                        swinging
                                        block-piling

Close your eyes to listen for sounds outside
                                        inside the room
  Can you hear your own breathing?
Maybe the teacher will make some special sounds
                              for you to name

When the teacher sings your name
Sing it back the same way
She'll know you brought your ears to school
and your voice

      Sing songs with words
                    without words
                              to tell
                                        a way to move
                                        a story
                                        how you feel

Play *Follow the Leader*
    with a friend facing you
        move parts of yourself
          the other person does the same thing
    in a line
        going everywhere in the room
          everybody has a turn to be leader
    Ask the teacher to sing or play
                    go or stop as the music does
Do what the words of the song tell you
                    ("Clap/tap/jump Jim-a-long")
Make some music to tell yourself
                    somebody else
                              what you want to do
                              how you feel

In 1961, J. McVickers Hunt attacked the notion that intelligence is totally predetermined at birth and presented evidence that experience could indeed modify intellectual ability. He suggested that ways could be found to govern children's encounters with their environ-

Music-Movement in the Total Curriculum

2. Concepts of Space and Time
   a. Learning shapes and forms
   b. Spatial perspective
   c. The notion of time

Move different parts of yourself
   Where are your hinges?

Make your arm
         head
         hips
         shoulders
               go in circles when you hear the song
                                 about the wheel
How big
      small
      can you make yourself?
Can you be a ball
         straight line on the floor?
         How many straight lines make a square
                                             triangle?
Make a square
         triangle
            on the floor with friends
   Can you make the shapes of letters?
Move parts of yourself
         sitting
         lying on the floor
         standing
               in many different directions
                  alone
                  with a friend
Move about the room without bumping another person
                                 the furniture
                                 the walls
Is there enough room to stretch your arms to
be an airplane?
                  Bank your arms to avoid bumping
Move fast—tiny steps
      slow—giant steps
            Listen inside you to find the beat that fits
Make little
      big
         steps
      Listen to your feet
      Let your hands clap the same way
Sing a part of a song
            Let your feet do it
            listen to how the words fit the melody
         clap as you move
         clap instead of moving
Sing a song that goes up a musical ladder
   Show how the song goes using your hand
                                 whole self
         Where will you have to begin?
Know which verse
         part
            comes next when you sing
                  hear
                        your favorite songs
      even when each verse adds something and you have to
                  think backwards! (cumulative songs)
Play the drum for the game of Go-Stop
      Make some of the go parts very short
                        longer

ments, especially during the early days of their development, to bring about a faster rate of intellectual development and even a substantially higher intellectual capacity.[3] Three years later, Benjamin Bloom published the results of a long-range study of intelligence that substantiated Hunt's view.[4]

Government-sponsored Head Start Programs for prekindergartners, begun in 1965, placed the main emphasis on cognitive development. Compensatory projects featured opportunities for rich sensory experiences with colors and shapes, verbalization of concepts, and development of the child's self-confidence in learning. Ellis Evans has listed some thirty-odd "Principal Preprimary Programs for Young Children," pointing out that most of them represent a strong cognitive-language development orientation.[5] The same emphasis prevails in the ten federally-funded Preschool Programs in Compensatory Education.[6]

An obvious question arises: How is continuity in education to be guaranteed through the school years and beyond? During the 1960s, scholars and practitioners gave considerable attention to the conceptual approach. The basic concepts of various disciplines were suggested as structures around and through which continuous growth could take place. These structures could form pragmatic foundations for the broadening and deepening of knowledge in all disciplines. Use of such a structure of concepts was shown to permit greater comprehension, better memory, more adequate transfer, and continuity through the years of formal and informal education.[7] In the now-classic quotation, Jerome Bruner hypothesized that "any subject can be taught effectively in some intellectually honest form to any child at any stage of development."[8] Especially in work with children of the poor, early childhood specialists were challenged to critique and revise their approaches to subject matter disciplines and also to question the validity of traditional IQ testing.

A New View of Intelligence

We have moved away from older norms (operations easily identified and analyzed in verbal terms), and we are now more likely to view intelligence as the capacity for knowledge and understanding, especially as applied to the handling of novel situations, and the capacity for the higher forms of thought. This broader view incorporates those characteristics once particularly associated with creativity—flexibility, fluency, divergent thinking, originality, and imagination.

Of particular significance to this newer look are the comprehensive studies headed by Burton White. These studies are concerned with the development of competence in young children; they identify the ingredients in children's successful coping with themselves and others. Choosing to study a broader range of early development, White used a "mongrel" definition in the form of a list of distinguishing abilities of competence in three- to six-year-old children. (He seems to prove meanwhile that from ten to eighteen months of age is the crucial time span in the development of these abilities.) This list of abilities is important because it dramatizes the pervasive interactions of social, motivational, and intellectual development. [9]

Similar features are a part of the open classroom concept. After making headlines as a British import, the term has come to mean many different things to different people. The philosophy is by no means revolutionary. Good early childhood teachers have long known that children have unique styles and speeds of learning, that a carefully designed environment can encourage individual involvement, and that diversity of personalities and levels of sophistication can make important contributions to dynamic and intriguing learning situations. [10] They know that motivation is not a separate ingredient of learning, but that it is woven into the individualization and resultant total involvement of the child in the learning challenge. "Total" in this

---

Music-Movement in the Total Curriculum

3. Beginning Logical Concepts
 a. Logical classification
 b. concepts of relationship

Hear that certain instrument sounds belong together
                which ones ring
                            knock
                            rattle
                which ones are made of metal
                                        wood
                            have rattle-y parts
Move yourself to the music showing when it changes from
                                    fast to slow
                                    slow to fast
                        from
                                    soft to loud
                                    loud to soft
                        from
                                    smooth to jerky
                                    jerky to smooth
            Keep asking yourself
                            how does it make you feel?
                            what does it make you do?
Put the bells in a row just the way the scale song goes
Make five beats on the drum sounding
                            from soft to loud
                            from loud to soft
Recognize your favorite songs
            even when
                the words are missing
                you hear only the ending
                                middle part
                                beginning (so easy!)

---

case means thinking and feeling and doing, interrelatedly, in open-ended, nonthreatening experiences. For these reasons, music-movement activities deserve top billing.

There is considerable evidence that all classroom teachers make on-the-spot curricular decisions as they face their students, although they rarely analyze their own behavior in this regard. What are the alternatives when the lesson plan doesn't work and the children become restless or disruptive? Some teachers continue doggedly by encouraging the "eager-to-satisfy-the-teacher" children to make the sounds and actions expected of them; the uninvolved, who are forced to be quiet, often become frustrated and build up negative feelings about learning. Other teachers dis-

Music-Movement in the Total Curriculum

4. The Growth of Reasoning Skills
   a. Understanding cause and effect
   b. Reasoning by association
   c. Reasoning by inference

Hold the triangle carefully by the cord
                                             play it gently
                    Do you like to hear the sound?
Hold the triangle itself
                    play it again
                    What happens?
                    What other instruments have sounds that ring for a while
                                                     and fade away?
                    Can you stop the sound if you want to?
                                             How?
Make the drum sound softer
                    louder
                            knowing how to make it happen
Go with the music showing how it is
                                    soft
                                    loud
                                        slow
                                        fast
                                              smooth
                                              jerky
            Can your face
                    body
                            show how the music makes you feel?
Play the *Echo Game* singing
                    clapping
                            making the echo
                                    exactly the same
                                    a bit different
                        listen to tell when it is
                                    exactly the same
                                    different
                        can you tell *how* it is different?
Play the *Naming Game*
                                remembering to keep your eyes closed
                                                     (covered)
            Can you tell
                    who is singing?
                    what instrument is being played?
Pretend there is a tremendous clock on the floor
            walk around it
                    clockwise
                    counterclockwise
            sing a song as you walk
                change directions when the song tells you to
                                             (phrases)

card the prepared plans and substitute an activity that was previously found to please and involve the whole class, but that has no particular objective except to keep control.

New Approaches in the Classroom

There is much that the teacher can learn from analyzing long-range objectives and trying to project what strategies will work. However, exciting and workable lesson plans are very difficult to write, and the most carefully devised plan is subject to detours and delays if one is to take cues from children's responses. Many teachers admit that they give hastily made, "warmed-over" lesson plans to their supervisors in accordance with job requirements, but that they do not use these plans in the classroom.

A teacher can decide to take another approach, based on the special need for moment-to-moment decisions when interacting with children. Instead of nervous planning *before* school, the teacher makes brief entries in a log as soon as possible *after* the experiences, projecting possibilities for the next day's learning. This plan makes longer-range demands; it requires that the teacher learn a repertoire of songs and music games, adding to them constantly. (Keen observation of children's free play afford valuable insights into their growing and changing interests.) The teacher prepares a list of the basic concepts of the elements of music and asks, "What can happen to the sounds to make you feel the way you do?" Comparative concepts are the easiest to handle: loud-soft, fast-slow, high-low, going up-going down, and same-different.[11] Finally, and most importantly, there is a need for a dependable structure. What will it be?

Because the most individual responses are apt to be in the emotional and physical realms, the common focus can be on the areas of intellectual development. A guide in the form of an outline of these intellectual areas encourages more personal, more individual responses. (Teachers are familiar with the terms used, from child development studies and from curriculum work in other subjects.) Following such a guide, the teacher can more easily see that music-movement activities are, or can become, basic experiences in the child's total growth experience.

Obviously, any clear outline can be used, and the number of appropriate activities is infinite. There will be many ways to organize materials because the areas often overlap. The teacher interacts with one child, a small group, or the whole class. Specific music-movement activities will evolve from other experiences, real or vicarious, as in storybooks or from television.

Pervading all suggestions and guidelines should be the reminder that music is organized sounds in time for the purpose of human expression. Music expression must not be compromised, even temporarily, to learn words or practice a skill. The young child is learning all the time; he or she can only assume that such unmusical drills are supposed to be music. Ways must be found to accomplish these necessary aspects without deviating from authentic music expression.

Music, by its very nature, encourages personal responses—both physical and emotional. Thus, broad planning for intellectual growth promotes teacher confidence even as it encourages flexibility, improvisation, and dynamic interaction in the classroom. What a joy it can be to watch young children involved in these open-ended activities, learning to deal with themselves, seeing inside themselves, and using their own consciousness and their own imagination.

Notes

1. Although a few early childhood curriculum guides have focused on developing cognitive concepts of the elements of music, the activities described are usually teacher-directed, and thus they do not guarantee the children's affective involvement.
2. See P. Phenix, "The Play Element in Education," *Educational Forum* 29 (March 1965): 197–

306; and S. G. Moore and S. Kilmer, *Contemporary Pre-School Education: A Program for Young Children* (New York: John Wiley & Sons. Inc., 1973).

3. J. M. Hunt, *Intelligence and Experience* (New York: The Ronald Press Company, 1961).

4. B. S. Bloom, *Stability and Change in Human Characteristics* (New York: John Wiley & Sons, 1964).

5. E. Evans, *Contemporary Influences in Early Childhood Education* (New York: Holt, Rinehart and Winston, 1971).

6. See the series of ten pamphlets called *It Works: Pre-School Program in Compensatory Education* (Washington, DC: U.S. Government Printing Office).

7. J. Bruner, *The Process of Education* (New York: Vintage Books, 1963).

8. Bruner, *The Process of Education*, 33.

9. B. L. White, J. C. Watts, et al., *Experience and Environment: Major Influences on the Development of the Young Child*, vol. I (Englewood Cliffs, NJ: Prentice Hall, 1973).

10. M. Brearley, ed., *The Teaching of Young Children: Some Applications of Piaget's Learning Theory* (New York: Schocken Books, 1970).

11. For a more extensive list, see F. W. Aronoff, *Music and Young Children* (New York: Holt, Rinehart and Winston, 1969), 22–25.

Frances Webber Aronoff is professor emerita of music and music education at New York University in New York City and currently advises in the Gallatin Division of the university.

Music educators have long "networked" with other early childhood professionals. Many articles printed in the NAEYC and ACEI journals have provided music education information to the larger audience of caregivers and classroom teachers. In this article, Dorothy McDonald and Jonny Ramsey provide various information as to the scope and content of a total music program for young children. In addition, the authors share specific information, validated with research sources, regarding such topics as the child's singing skills and appropriate teaching techniques. The authors consider questions regarding children's singing such as "At what pitch levels can young children sing most comfortably? Are there certain melodic patterns which children sing easily? What kinds of musical experiences could help them achieve accuracy and 'tunefulness' in singing?" The content of this article provides today's educators with easily accessible resource information such as vocal-range expectations for young children, infants through five-year-olds.

Awakening the Artist

Music for Young Children

BY DOROTHY T. MCDONALD WITH JONNY H. RAMSEY

 visitor to any center for early childhood education in this country would probably hear music of some kind. Children like to sing; they like to play musical instruments; they like to listen to records. Teachers of young children generally include musical activities daily for the pleasure these activities give, for the release from tension they can often provide, and for aid in developing cognitive skills in many curricular areas. Most teachers, however, find it necessary to proceed by instinct; there is little information about the kinds of musical experiences that are appropriate for the young child, the methods and techniques that might be helpful in planning musical activities, or the criteria that might be applied when choosing musical materials for young children. From study of the research and theory about the musical development of young children, we have formulated the following guidelines for teachers to use in planning for one of children's most meaningful human experiences—responding to and making music.

Learning to Listen

From studies of infant responses to music, a first guideline seems appropriate: *Music should be included daily for infants as well as for older children. The presence of music, whether through recordings or the teacher's singing or playing, can awaken early responses to musical sound and can encourage infants to learn to listen.*

Noy described music as an auditory channel of communication and emotional exchange between the infant and the outside world.[1] McDonald also suggested music's importance in the emotional well-being of children; she wrote about children selecting a familiar song or composition, heard in the home, as a transition tune—something of the child's world that helps the child alleviate anxieties and makes acquaintances with the outside world more pleasurable.[2] Michel reported that children receive and re-

Dorothy T. McDonald with Jonny H. Ramsey, "Awakening the Artist: Music for Young Children," *Young Children* 33, no. 2 (January 1978): 187–93. *Young Children* is a publication of the National Association for the Education of Young Children (NAEYC).

spond to music at a very early age—"at two months [an infant] will lie motionless, with fixed attention to the sound of singing or playing of an instrument."[3] It would appear that musical experiences can and should be purposefully planned even for infants.

A baby seldom is thought of as a singer. Ostwald, however, noted that even infants attempt to vocalize musical intervals at an early age.[4] Described as a period of vocal contagion, this stage can begin before the second half of the first year. He cited studies by Mead of cultures where nurses are specifically instructed to encourage infants' vocalizations by mimicking the babies' sounds.

Thus, the presence of music in the first year, when the child is primarily a receiver of music, appears to be an important prerequisite to participation in the music-making process. Receiving evolves to sound-making and, subsequently, to music-making.

Learning to Sing

As young children become interested in participating in making music, certain questions arise. At what pitch levels can they sing most comfortably? Are there certain melodic patterns that children sing easily? What kinds of musical experiences could help them achieve accuracy and "tunefulness" in singing?

A second guideline, based on studies of young children's singing, is: *Singing should be included in the daily activities of preschool children, but expectations of achievement should be based upon knowledge of the developmental nature of this ability. Songs for classroom use should be chosen with careful consideration of tonality, range, melodic configurations, and vocal developmental stages of the children.*

Around the age of two, before many children will attempt to join in group singing, *chanting,* a form of spontaneous singing, is often heard among children at play. Many children experiment with familiar word patterns by giving them a tune—*language-related chants*—while others like to repeat a melodic pattern, experimenting with tonal sounds.[5] Often chants do not seem rhythmically related to the physical activity they accompany. The melodic patterns reported by observers appear to be those commonly found in songs of the child's culture.[6] Ascending and descending scale patterns, falling minor thirds, fourths, and fifths seem to be frequently used intervals. One of the most commonly heard melodic patterns in play activities is the familiar teasing chant—two falling minor thirds separated by the upper neighbor of the higher tone (*sol-mi-la-sol-mi*). The familiar song, "Rain, Rain, Go Away" uses this pattern for the entire song. Perhaps musical conversations can be created by teacher and child using this common pattern.

At what pitch levels do young children sing easily? Cooper has reported that two-year-old children seem to sing most comfortably in a range from D_4 to A_4 (with middle C being C_4)—a range of five diatonic tones above middle C.[7] Songs such as "Go Tell Aunt Rhody," the chorus of "Jingle Bells," "Twinkle, Twinkle, Little Star" (six tones), and "This Old Man" (six tones), long favorites with children, can be pitched to fit comfortably in this range; these songs also employ the melodic patterns cited above.

As children grow, their vocal range expands. Simons reported, in the spontaneous singing of children thirty-one months to nine years of age, a usable range from C_4 to C_5 in twins and $A\flat_3$ to B_4 in singletons.[8] Kirkpatrick reported that the range used most frequently by five-year-old children extended from G_3 to $B\flat_4$.[9] Over half the children tested had extensive ranges from F_3 to E_5; however, approximately 20 percent had limited ranges from B_3 to $F\sharp_4$. From a comparison of these ranges, it seems that even for children who have wide singing ranges, tones in the relatively low range below middle C become usable as soon as, or before, those in a relatively higher range (above A_4 or B_4).

When learning songs (imitative singing), however, the requirements of matching tones and words result in more restricted ranges.[10] Drexler found that the most frequently used range of three- to six-year-old children was from C_4 to D_5, but that the lower pitches were sung more easily.[11] Young and Smith reported similar findings.[12]

These researchers also reported certain sequential stages in the development of tuneful singing. While great individual differences exist among children, and no age seems significantly related to each stage, teachers may observe the following growth pattern. First, young children attempt to use the range of their speaking voices to reproduce songs. Next, they might exhibit inconsistent melodic direction. Gradually gaining vocal control, they may become accurate directionally, but inaccurate in interval reproduction. The hoped-for final stage is the accurate reproduction of a melody within a given tonality.

Maturation appears to be the most significant factor in range development; Boardman and Smith found that first-grade children who had received early group training in singing, as well as those who had not, had more difficulty with upper-range accuracy than with lower tones.[13]

When choosing songs for beginning group singing, teachers might be advised to include many songs in ranges from approximately B_3 to A_4. Perhaps the concept of tuneful singing—important to all subsequent musical experiences—may be formed more easily in songs of this limited range.

Hermanson suggested that teachers teach songs using voice rather than piano; in her study, pitch accuracy was best when the children imitated a woman's voice and worst with a piano.[14] One finding of a larger study by Sargeant and Roche drew attention to the matter of pitching songs in a consistent manner (each time a song is sung, it is sung in the same tonality).[15] In their study, children three or four years of age tended to remember and reproduce songs at the same pitch levels in which the songs were learned.

Studies of techniques for helping children discriminate melodic intervals—a skill important in singing accuracy—provide a third guideline. *Visual, verbal, and motor cues may be effective in helping young children develop concepts of melodic interval and direction.*

Yendovitskaya designed a pitch-discrimination training program for three-and four-year-old children in which the subjects were taught to represent melodic intervals with matching arm amplitude; wide intervals were represented with arms far apart, narrow intervals with arms close together. He found that the physical representation was prerequisite for these children's successful identification of paired pitches as same or different.[16] Repina trained children to associate low and high pitches with pictures of large and small animals. Williams used the piano keyboard as a visual cue in helping young children acquire concepts of melodic direction (tones moving "upstairs" or "downstairs").[17]

In a similar manner, a teacher may provide visual cues, such as moving the hands up and down with the tones of a song or playing the melody on songbells held vertically. The inclusion of songs whose lyrics describe direction ("number songs" might fit in this category) or suggest directional physical movement ("I Put My Arms Up High") can provide experiences with the concept of melodic direction.

Learning to Move

To a young child, melody and movement are closely related; studies of children's spontaneous singing have shown that songs often grow out of motor activities. Studies by Greenberg, Romanek, and Belyayeva-Ekzemplyarskaya show that concepts of beat, tempo, and dynamics may develop before those of pitch, melody, harmony, and form. However, most young children need experience with rhythmic movement before they are successful in duplicating or synchronizing movement with music.[18] One of the first spontaneous rhythmic activities among children is producing a *beat*.[19] These regular, unaccented pulsations are quite fast in tempo ($\downarrow$ = 120 to $\downarrow$ = 176), and little attempt is made to synchronize them with those of other children.[20] When accents appear, they are often irregular and experimental in nature. At three years of age, the child's ability to synchronize beat with music for a controlled duration of time begins to develop; at age four, interest in dramatizing ideas in music appears; at age five, most children are able to march, clap, and otherwise keep time with music at relatively fast tempos.[21]

Training does not seem to improve these skills significantly; maturation is the most important factor. Therefore, a fourth guideline for planning rhythmic experiences might be expressed: *Rhythmic activities should start with exploration rather than duplication. Synchronization training is less important than the opportunity to explore movement and rhythm.*

Fingerplays, action songs, and musical games provide many exploratory experiences with rhythmic expression. Songs such as "This Old Man," and "Jim Along Josie," "In and Out the Window," and "Little Rabbit in the Wood" are but a few that can be used to encourage rhythmic expression. Many recent recordings for young children also encourage creative exploratory movement rather than synchronization with a beat or pattern. Hap Palmer's *Creative Movement and Rhythmic Expression* (Educational Activities, Inc.) provides delightful exploratory experiences with rhythmic movement.

Learning to Hear

Music is an aural art, and the development of listening skills is one of the most important objectives of any music program. What kinds of music attract young children? How can teachers encourage attentive listening?

Alford reported that young children show a greater degree of response to music that is predominantly rhythmic or melodic rather than that which is harmonic or dissonant.[22] Singing attempts have been reported in children as young as four to six months of age.[23] From six months to one year, babies try out clearly audible musical intervals, usually within a range of three to five tones.[24]

McDonald and Schuckert found that when children were allowed to choose between a jazz selection and a classical selection, jazz was the preferred choice.[25] However, some children showed increased interest in the classical selection over a period of exposure time.

Studies by Fullard; Greer, Dorow, and Hanser; and Allen revealed very young children's ability to learn to identify orchestral instruments by matching pictures of the instruments with their sound when played.[26] Instruments identified by three-, four-, and five-year-old children included violin, clarinet, cello, flute, viola, French horn, bassoon, oboe, and trumpet. Young children appear to be discriminating in selecting an appropriate timbre, also, when choosing percussive instruments for rhythmic activities.[27] Such information suggests a guideline for planning listening experiences: *Music listening experiences may be included as an important part of an early childhood music curriculum. Discrimination tasks, including identification of individual or families of instruments may be appropriate and may increase interest in listening to many different kinds of music.*

The Bowmar albums, including *The Young Listener;* records developed for identification of instruments; and selected albums from the Folkways recordings of music from other cultures are valuable sources.

Learning to Learn

A final guideline is formulated from studies in which music was used as an aid to cognitive development in other curriculum areas: *Music and movement may be useful in motivating and helping children to acquire verbal concepts, oral communication, and aural discrimination skills.*

Because music is a pleasurable and nonthreatening experience for most children, it can sometimes be used to help children with special needs feel comfortable while learning. Seybold, a speech therapist, reported that a remedial program that included singing conversations, and singing games that required primary color identification and provided experiences with verbal concepts such as "up and down," yielded significant posttest gains in language development test scores for normal, but speech-delayed, children.[28] Greenberg and Pruitt and Steele developed programs for children in Head Start classrooms, and have cited significant gains, not only in music concept formation, but also in cognitive skills such as right-left discrimination, color identification, counting, and body image.[29]

In similar fashion, a teacher may use familiar, favorite songs to enhance developmental skills. The use of substitute words in many familiar songs can provide reinforcement for skills such as color identification ("Mary Wore a Red Dress," for example).

What can be said can also be sung. A teacher can initiate singing conversations using tonal chants (perhaps the familiar descending minor third *sol-mi*) to encourage children to formulate thoughts into phrases and sentences. Music may help these kinds of experiences become enjoyable and successful games.

Music for the young child should be planned for more than tension release or leisure-time entertainment. Developing sensitivity to one's world—perceptual, cognitive, and emotional—is an important goal for the education of young children. For "if we awaken the artist...at a tender age, when [the child] is so receptive to all beauty, then [the child's] later life will be incomparably more fulfilled and enriched."

Notes

1. P. Noy, "The Development of Musical Ability," *The Psychoanalytic Study of the Child* 23 (1968): 332–47.
2. M. McDonald, "Transitional Tunes and Musical Development," *The Psychoanalytic Study of the Child* 25 (1970): 503–20.
3. P. Michel, "The Optimum Development of Musical Abilities in the First Years of Life," *Psychology of Music* 1, no. 2 (June 1973): 17.
4. P. F. Ostwald, "Musical Behavior in Early Childhood," *Developmental Medicine and Child Neurology* 15, no. 1 (February 1973): 367–75.
5. G. M. Simons, "Comparisons of Incipient Music Responses Among Very Young Twins and Singletons," *Journal of Research in Music Education* 12, no. 3 (Fall 1964): 212–26.
6. G. Scheihing, "A Study of the Spontaneous Rhythmic Activities of Preschool Children," in *Music Therapy 1951*, ed. E. G. Gilliland (Lawrence, KS: Allen Press, 1952), 188–89.
7. R. M. Cooper, "Music and the Two-Year-Olds," *Music Journal* 31, no. 1 (January 1973): 13.
8. Simons, "Comparisons of Incipient Music Responses."
9. W. F. Kirkpatrick, "Relationships Between the Singing Ability of Prekindergarten Children and Their Home Musical Environment," *Dissertation Abstracts* 23, no. 3 (September 1962): 886.
10. A. T. Jersild and S. F. Bienstock, *Development of Rhythm in Young Children* (New York: Columbia University, 1935).
11. E. N. Drexler, "A Study of the Development of the Ability to Carry a Melody at the Preschool Level," *Child Development* 9 (March-December 1938): 319–32.
12. W. T. Young, "An Investigation of the Singing Abilities of Kindergarten and First Grade Children in East Texas," (Bethesda, MD: ERIC Document Reproduction Service, 1971) ED 069 431; and R. B. Smith, "The Effect of Group Vocal Training on the Singing Ability of Nursery School Children," *Journal of Research in Music Education* 11, no. 2 (Fall 1963): 137–41.

13. E. L. Boardman, "An Investigation of the Effect of Preschool Training on the Development of Vocal Accuracy in Young Children," *Bulletin of the Council for Research in Music Education* 11 (Fall 1967): 46–49; and R. B. Smith, *Music in the Child's Education* (New York: Ronald Press, 1970).

14. L. W. Hermanson, "An Investigation of the Effects of Timbre on Simultaneous Vocal Pitch Acuity of Young Children," *Dissertation Abstracts International* 32, no. 7 (January 1972): 3558-A.

15. D. Sergeant and S. Roche, "Perceptual Shifts in the Auditory Information Processing of Young Children," *Psychology of Music* 1, no. 2 (June 1973): 39–48.

16. T. V. Yendovitskaya, "Development of Sensation and Perception," in *The Psychology of Preschool Children*, ed. A. V. Zaporzhets and D. B. Elkonin, trans. J. Shybut and S. Simon (Cambridge, MA: MIT Press, 1971), 1–64.

17. H. M. Williams, "Techniques of Measurement in the Developmental Psychology of Music," in *Studies in Child Welfare: The Measurement of Musical Development*, ed. G. D. Stoddard (Iowa City: University of Iowa, 1932): 11–31.

18. M. Greenberg, "A Preliminary Report of the Effectiveness of a Music Curriculum with Preschool Head Start Children," *Bulletin of the Council for Research in Music Education* 29 (Summer 1972): 13–16; and M. L. Romanek, "A Self-Instructional Program for Musical Concept Development in Pre-school Children," *Journal of Research in Music Education* 22, no. 2 (Summer 1974): 129–35.

19. R. Shuter, *The Psychology of Musical Ability* (London: Methuen and Co., 1968).

20. Scheihing, "A Study of the Spontaneous Rhythmic Activities"; and Simons, "Comparisons of Incipient Music Responses."

21. H. Christianson, *Bodily Movement of Young Children in Relation to Rhythm in Music* (New York: Columbia University, 1938); and Jersild and Bienstock, *Development of Rhythm.*

22. D. L. Alford, "Emergence and Development of Music Responses in Preschool Twins and Singletons: A Comparative Study," *Journal of Research in Music Education* 19, no. 2 (Summer 1971): 222–27.

23. Michel, "The Optimum Development of Musical Abilities."

24. Shuter, *The Psychology of Musical Ability.*

25. R. L. McDonald and R. F. Schuckert, "An Attempt to Modify the Musical Preferences of Preschool Children," *Journal of Research in Music Education* 16, no. 1 (Spring 1968): 39–44.

26. W. G. Fullard, Jr., "Operant Training of Aural Musical Discriminations with Preschool Children." *Journal of Research in Music Education* 15, no. 3 (Fall 1967): 201–09; R. D. Greer, L. Dorow, and S. Hanser, "Music Discrimination Training and the Music Selection Behavior of Nursery and Primary Level Children," *Bulletin of the Council for Research in Music Education* 35 (Winter 1973): 30–43; and E. B. Allen, "A Study of Perception of Instrumental Tone Color by Children of Nursery School Age," Master's thesis, University of Kansas, 1959.

27. Shuter, *The Psychology of Musical Ability.*

28. C. D. Seybold, "The Value and Use of Music Activities in the Treatment of Speech-Delayed Children," *Journal of Music Therapy* 8 (Fall 1971): 102–10.

29. Greenberg, "A Preliminary Report"; and H. Pruitt and A. L. Steele, "Music by Head Start Teachers for the Educationally Disadvantaged," *American Music Teacher* 20, no. 6 (June-July 1971): 29–30, 37.

Dorothy T. McDonald is professor of music education in the Division of Curriculum and Instruction of the University of Iowa in Iowa City, and a former music teacher in Iowa, Illinois, and North Carolina.
Jonny H. Ramsey teaches K–5 music at the Seven Hills Elementary School in Rhome, Texas, and is a part-time instructor of music at Texas Christian University.

❖

SECTION 3

A New Look

Topics for Today's Concerns in
Early Childhood Music Education

Four specific concerns have been identified as greatly important to those who must shape and guide effective programs in today's early childhood learning settings:

- meeting the needs of young children who are educationally at risk;
- including developmentally appropriate multicultural musical experiences in the play experiences of young children;
- acquiring further insights as to the child's thinking skills; and
- exploring options for adequately assessing the musical growth of the young learner.

In this section, four authors were invited to generate new articles relating to these topics. Their expertise and findings have proven to be most insightful and will be of great value as we continue to pursue excellence in music education for young children.

Metacognition! Critical thinking! Creative thinking! All are processes that are currently being studied and applied by those developing curricula in education. Few educators have attempted to address these concerns in their relationship to how the very young child processes information. Elayne Achilles defines the term metacognition and explores the role of language in its development. Achilles explains that researchers define the child's global awareness of reading as "postliteracy" (children become postliterate before learning to read, in other words, they understand why people read before learning how). The author asks, "Does this indicate that preschool children might also require 'postmusicality' skills before they can understand their involvement in music?" The article continues with a discussion of the differences in critical and creative thinking. Open-ended creative teaching strategies are included as a means of describing appropriate practice necessary to assist the child in obtaining optimum musical dispositions.

Current Perspectives on Young Children's Thinking
Implications for Preschool Music Education

BY ELAYNE ACHILLES

n order to make informed decisions about developmentally appropriate curricula, music educators frequently consult research in educational psychology. How children think, learn, and grow in early childhood is critical, since mental operations seem to change more rapidly during this stage of development than any other. Piaget's theories of mental development have provided the framework for the formation of instructional strategies of most preschool programs and have remained unchallenged until recently. Partly because of new measurement techniques, researchers have shown that the young child's abilities may have been underestimated. Flavell has reported that young infants can perceive and retain more complex and abstract patterns of information processing, putting into question the premise that the newborn is a blank slate upon which all perceptions are drawn.[1] If infants develop their perceptual capabilities earlier than previously assumed, what implications arise for the education of young children?

Educational psychologists have examined the development of knowledge structures in different ways, resulting in comparatively new perspectives on cognition known as metacognition, critical thinking, and creative thinking. Music educators have used these terms in describing appropriate classroom practice but few have addressed the area of preschool music education.[2] This chapter focuses on current research in the development of metacognition and creativity in children ages two to five years and how the findings may be applied to developing curricula in early childhood music education.

Metacognition

Three-year-old Kevin is riding in the child seat of the family car when Dad asks him to look at the trees. Kevin soon starts chanting the word "trees," raising and lowering the pitch of his voice, extending the "e" vowel in a melismatic way, repeating melodic intervals, and adding other words and parts of known songs. Kevin has just created a song improvisation. Is Kevin aware that he is making music? Does he monitor and adjust his singing as he performs? The idea of being aware of our thinking as we perform tasks and then using this awareness to control what we are doing is known as metacognition.[3] The prefix "meta" derives from the Greek meaning "after" or "beyond," signifying a higher level of consciousness. Metacognition refers to the ability to reflect on one's own thinking processes and to regulate them for more efficient learning.

Very few studies have been conducted concerning the metacognitive abilities of preschool children. Pramling showed that children progress developmentally through stages of metacognitive ways of thinking.[4] She concluded that most children under the age of four years have no idea that they are learning. At about four years, most children have the idea of learning "to do" or knowing *what* they are doing. Very few preschool children connected learning with knowing *how* they think about what they are doing, and no preschool children showed an awareness of thinking about their own thinking. As an example of the different levels of thought, Pramling suggested that a child thinking about why it is raining would not be asking a metacognitive question, but if the child gives attention to how they think about why it rains, the question becomes metacognitive.

Children who have a functional view of an activity have superior performance over those who see learning solely as a school activity. In math learning, Doverborg showed that children who could talk about situations related to the importance of knowing math ("so my brother won't cheat me on sweets") succeeded more than children who said it was necessary to learn math because it was a school subject.[5] In studying how

children learn to read, Mikkelson found that children who stated a personal meaning in learning to read (that is, as a means of communication) learned to read more proficiently than children who saw reading as a technical process (that is, sounding out letters).[6] Mikkelson referred to the more global awareness of reading as "postliteracy." She concluded that it is possible for children to become postliterate before learning to read, in other words, to understand *why* people read before learning *how*. Developing postliteracy skills before learning to read may be an essential metacognitive function. What "postmusicality" skills might be required for preschool children to understand their involvement in music? How can teachers encourage development of this type of metacognitive musical awareness?

Language in the Development of Metacognition

The development of self-regulatory behavior through language may be an important form of metacognition in preschool children. In an experimental study of adult-child interactions, Kontos asked parents to give verbal directions to their children (ages 3–5) to help them put a puzzle together.[7] However, in the control group, the parents were told to offer their children only praise and encouragement without direct instruction. She found that the children working with praise alone seemed to improve as much as those whose parents gave verbal directions. It seems that the child's problem-solving performance was as effective through his or her self-regulation as it was with help from parents. This study indicates that the way adults use language with children may be important in the child's self-regulatory behavior and that very young children have some ability to regulate their own behavior.

Although children do not seem to benefit from adults' direct verbal instructions, they appear to voluntarily regulate their own behavior through other forms of verbal communication by adults. In an earlier study of preschool children's responses to music, Metz found that two- three-, and four-year-old children's movement responses to music increased when teachers described the children's actions in musical terms. [8] By semantically labeling the musical responses of children according to their qualitative properties (for example, "Tommy you're playing the drum fast"), teachers elicited additional qualitative responses, such as playing slow, alternating between fast and slow, or exploring other elements of music. It has been shown in language acquisition research that children search for semantic rules rather than resort to trial and error. [9] In seeking the meaning of words, children look for relational words that are linked to form contrasting pairs, such as big/small. In music instruction, the use of the elements of music can be described by bipolar opposites: loud/soft, fast/slow, high pitch/low pitch, same/different, long sounds/short sounds, and so on. In the Metz study, children voluntarily incorporated the teacher's semantic labels when making verbal and movement responses to the music.

Semantic labeling of children's responses to music in the form of contrasting qualities of musical elements may be one of the strongest links to developing postmusicality skills in young children. Adults can assist children in learning the specialized language of music as the child explores and manipulates sounds. By exploring all the possible responses along the continuum of any selected element, such as fast/slow, the child gains an essential understanding of that particular element of music. By using the specialized language of music, the child is able to determine the fundamental nature of music and its critical elements, distinguishing the concept of music from other concepts. By exploring and experimenting with the elements of music, the child grasps an awareness of some fundamental properties of music.

Although semantic labeling of musical elements helps young children attain an understanding of the fundamental nature of music, research has shown that young children can understand and solve problems by doing, while being unable to discuss or even be aware of their own actions. [10] In other words, children can make decisions without making verbalizations. We frequently see three-year-olds experimenting with differences in tempo by playing fast on the drum for a few seconds, then playing slow. If the child were older, he or she might say, "I'm tired of playing fast so I think I'll play slow," or "I know what playing fast sounds like, I wonder what it sounds like to play slow?" It seems that the ability to regulate one's thinking in music occurs much sooner than the ability to reflect on (verbalize and be aware of) those musical thoughts.

Children's ability to define their musical explorations with words may be an important key in answering the question of what postmusicality skills are required for musical understanding. Preschool children appear to possess the ability to regulate their own musical behavior but do not naturally possess the ability to reflect on that behavior. Linking the child's musical explorations with the adult's semantic labeling may provide the path for burgeoning metacognitive awareness.

Creative Thinking

According to Marzano and colleagues, critical thinking is primarily evaluative and creative thinking is primarily generative. [11] The authors state that these two types of thinking complement each other and share many attributes. Critical thinking is defined as reasonable, reflective thinking that is focused on deciding what to believe or do. [12] It involves both dispositions, such as being open-minded, and abilities, such as asking questions, analyzing arguments, judging criteria, inferring, and generalizing conclusions. Pogonowski provides excellent examples of fostering critical thinking in music making and music listening strategies. [13]

The goal of creative thinking is output, according to Perkins. [14] Halpern describes creativity as the ability to form new combinations of ideas. [15] Current research supports the belief of Torrance that creativity can and should be taught. [16] Martin conducted research with prospective preschool teachers in a university class in order to increase their creative thinking skills and to use those principles to create teaching strategies for preschool children. [17] Using the Torrance Tests of Creative Thinking, Martin found that a majority of the preservice students showed gains in creative thinking as a result of training, and that consequently they used creative thinking skills in developing lesson plans for preschool children. These findings support the notion that in order to teach creatively, a teacher must be creative. How should preschool teachers be prepared to teach creatively?

Creative Behaviors

The paradox of language development is that it is governed by rules and at the same time is also creative. Speech forms have regular patterns but there are infinite ways to combine these patterns to create meaning. In the same way that children develop rule-bound and improvisational language skills, they naturally create music through a combination of rules and improvisation, such as the spontaneous song improvisation about trees performed by three-year-old Kevin while riding in the car, or by playing musical instruments. Teachers can encourage the wonder and exploration that accompanies this natural behavior by fostering the dispositions that underlie creativity, such as being open and avoiding closure. If teachers think of children as "putting out" knowledge rather than "consuming" knowledge, certain behaviors will be favored over others. For example, a disposition toward divergent behavior that considers several re-

sponses to a single idea might be preferred to convergent thinking that limits activity to a single response.

A preschool teacher may encourage the child to find several ways to play the xylophone rather than providing only one way for a child to respond. An exploratory behavior, where the child decides to place different objects on a drumhead to determine the different sounds, would be preferred to a directed behavior, where the teacher might ask the child to play the drum in a certain way at a certain time. An active response, such as having children respond with movement while listening to particular elements in the music, should be encouraged over passive responses, where the child hears music being played in the background during other activities.

Creative teaching strategies include many opportunities for children to respond at their own discretion rather than on command. Forming open questions aids that development. An example of an open question might be "How many ways can you find to go around the circle?" while a closed question might be "Can you skip around the circle?" Holistic approaches to creating music, as opposed to mastery approaches, help the child understand how the parts fit within the whole (the *Gestalt*). A holistic activity might be to encourage a child to find all the sounds that can be made on the violin strings, while in a mastery approach, the child would be directed to place the fingers correctly in first position, thereby limiting the child's focus. Student-directed activities develop personal responsibility for learning. A child pretending to be a famous singer, making up songs with a pretend microphone, directs his or her own behavior more than the child participating in a group sing-along.

Attempting to obtain closure too quickly can interfere with the creative process. For example, the teacher may want to finish a story in which the child is encouraged to make musical responses, instead of stopping the story when the child wishes to explore a multitude of musical responses elicited by the story. Creative teachers encourage unusual ideas. In exploring all the sounds a xylophone makes, a child might find an unusual sound by tapping two of the bars together or dumping all the bars on the floor at once, rather than conforming to typical responses.

Environments for Creative Behaviors

As shown in the examples above, many young children naturally engage in creative music making, whether by singing, playing instruments, or moving. Creative musical behaviors are self-regulatory and involve the kind of reflection that is a component of metacognition. Preschool environments can be specially designed to promote creative thinking in music. Typical of current practice, many preschools designate certain areas of the room for particular types of activities such as dramatic play, painting, wet/dry table, and book area. These learning centers may also include a music environment or learning center. As suggested by Andress, music environments can be structured much like the other learning centers in the preschool.[18] A primary goal for effective use is that music centers attract children to the area and stimulate music making. Children should be able to choose from a rich selection of quality music-making materials and to listen to a wide variety of music on high-quality stereo equipment. Since play is a reflection of what children are learning, an environment that allows for the elements of play, such as intrinsic motivation, freedom from external rules, exploratory behavior, active engagement, and pretense, is essential.

This kind of music-learning environment is based on free-choice participation, allowing for exploratory behavior based on the needs, interests, and ability of the child. The children direct their own activity by deciding how much time to spend in the area and how they will respond to the materials.

The role of the teacher is that of facilitator. As mentioned above, the teacher's most important task in developing the child's postmusicality is to use semantic labeling in describing the children's musical responses. Descriptions that label the child's music behavior in terms of the qualities of the elements of music provide a vocabulary that allows the child to achieve a fundamental understanding of the nature of music and to lay the foundation for additional creative behaviors. This kind of student-directed behavior fosters independent thinking and autonomous behavior, the hallmark of creativity and an important psychosocial need of all children.

Music activities for preschool children should be open ended and should focus on child norms rather than on adult norms. For example, in using a set of bells, a preschooler may find no meaning in classifying the bells according to pitch, but may find his or her own ways of organizing the sounds. A child at this age needs mastery of his or her own playthings more than mastery of pitch order.

Activities should also be general in nature, avoiding theme-specific strategies that limit divergent responses. For example, a child can explore sound more creatively by using the keyboard to make sound effects in a story rather than learning to play a specific song.

Since young children thrive on independent learning, teacher-directed group music activities such as circle time should be minimized in preschool. It is equally important to realize that music does and should take place beyond the music learning center. Teachers should observe and enter into children's rhythmic song improvisations on the playground or at snack time. Teachers should describe a child's rhythmic movements while running, walking, galloping, or working with equipment. Teachers should try to make up songs for every occasion; by doing so they enter into the spirit of play, which is an essential ingredient for creative thinking.

Collaborative Involvement in Young Children's Musicianship

Parents, educators, and administrators favor parental involvement in children's learning, but there is little consensus on what kind of involvement is most effective. Research has shown that students' achievement is enhanced by active parent involvement; however, parents' direct control techniques seemed to hamper children's cognitive development.[19] Research on math achievement has shown that children's self-perceptions of math ability appear to be influenced more by their parents' appraisals than by their own achievements.[20] The implications of this research point to the powerful influence of parent involvement on the attitudes, expectations, beliefs, and achievement of their children.

Most teachers do not know the best way to get parents involved in their children's education. In a survey of teacher educators, Chavkin and Williams found that teachers receive virtually no teacher training in parental involvement, a startling fact considering that the parent is the child's first teacher.[21] Further, many teachers have low expectations of how well parents can help their children learn. If preschool children should develop "postmusicality" skills, then it is essential that music educators, preschool teachers, and parents collaborate on that goal.

The Collaborative Model of Preschool Music Education

School treatment of special subjects such as music have evolved from the expert model to the collaborative consultation model. In the expert model, the music specialist provides music instruction directly to the students. In the collaborative model, every participant in the process "gives and receives information and alternately plays the expert and recipient roles in a forum where solution finding is jointly and equally shared among people with different knowledge and experience."[22] The outcome is enhanced, altered, and different from the original solutions that any team member would produce independently. All members of the team are perceived and treated as having needed expertise.

In the musical development of the preschool child, there are many team members, including parents, siblings, preschool teacher, and music specialist. Among these qualities are developing a shared belief system among all team members, learning to work in a group, releasing the role of expert in music to all team members, accepting other roles, and developing mutually owned outcomes.

Although very little research has specifically addressed the metacognitive abilities of preschool children, there appears to be some consensus on the thinking processes of preschool children. Studies indicate that very young children possess an important characteristic of metacognition, that of self-regulation. However, the ability to reflect on their own thinking and doing appears to be inchoate. Studies on the development of receptive and expressive language during preschool years points to the assertion that direct verbal instruction may not be an effective means of teaching at this stage of development. However, since children are mastering language at this time, other types of adult verbal communication with children may influence their semantic understanding of concepts.

It may be inferred from research that "postliteracy" functions as a metacognitive awareness in young children in which they understand the role and function of reading before actually learning how to read. Likewise, "postmusicality" may be considered a metacognitive awareness of music and how music differs from other concepts. We may find an important tool in helping children develop postmusicality awareness in semantic labeling of the expressive qualities of music.

Since the preschool child learns differently than the primary child, it is imperative that the "expert model" of music education instruction found extensively in public schools be replaced with the "collaborative model," in which the music specialist, preschool teacher, parents, and other adults share beliefs, attitudes, values, and roles of music teaching in the development of young children's thinking about music.

If it is true that young children develop cognitive and perceptual abilities earlier than previously assumed, how will early childhood education be affected? Will parents and teachers attempt to begin formal training earlier? Elkind refers to the trend toward beginning formal training at younger ages as the "superbaby syndrome."[23] By introducing academic skills too early, Katz suggests we risk undermining the child's disposition to engage in that activity.[24] She maintains that it is not useful to have skills if, in the process of acquiring them, the disposition to use them is lost. In terms of metacognition, musical dispositions may include postmusicality awareness, which encourages the young child to view music's function as well as music skills holistically.

Developing the notion of postmusicality may be a step toward providing the global awareness of music that children need to place their music-making experiences within a larger framework. Increasing the metacognitive awareness of the function of music as an expressive art may be more important than developing particular skills for which the child does not understand the purpose.

The literature on young children's thinking points to some essential considerations for music education. Since young children possess self-regulatory behavior at very early ages, it is important that direct instruction in early childhood music settings be avoided and experimentation and exploration be encouraged. At the same time, we must recognize the limited cognitive reflective capabilities of young children and their inchoate development of thought through language. Teachers should practice "semantic labeling" of musical elements, which helps children understand the critical elements of music and to reflect on their own music-making.

It is also essential that future early childhood music educators be prepared to articulate to parents and care-providers of preschool children the importance of maintaining nondirective roles when interacting musically with children. Also, music teachers should be prepared to exchange the expert model (or music teacher as specialist) to the collaborative model (or music teacher as a part of a team) when working with parents and teachers of preschool children. Future teachers trained to adopt these behaviors will enhance the nature of music-making with young children.

Notes

1. J. Flavell, *Cognitive Development* (Englewood Cliffs, NJ: Prentice Hall, 1985).
2. L. Pogonowski, "Developing Skills in Critical Thinking and Problem Solving," *Music Educators Journal* 73, no. 6 (1987): 37–41; L. Pogonowski, "Critical Thinking and Music Listening," *Music Educators Journal* 76, no. 1 (1989): 35–8; R. Erbes, *Elementary General Music: A Discipline-Based Review, Elementary Subjects Center Series No. 4* (East Lansing, MI: Michigan State University, East Lansing Institute for Research on Teaching, 1988); G. Greenberg, "Constructing Musical Knowledge," in *Arts and Learning SIG. Proceedings of the Annual Meeting of the American Educational Research Association*, ed. J. Koroscik and T. Barrett (Chicago, March 31–April 4, 1985): 90-99; W. May, *Understanding and Critical Thinking in Elementary Art and Music. Elementary Subjects Center Series No. 8* (East Lansing, MI: Michigan State University, East Lansing Institute for Research on Teaching, 1989); B. Alvarez, "Musical Thinking and the Young Child," in *Dimensions of Musical Thinking*, ed. E. Boardman (Reston, VA: Music Educators National Conference, 1989).

3. Flavell, *Cognitive Development*.

4. I. Pramling, "Developing Children's Thinking About Their Own Learning," *British Journal of Educational Psychology* 58 (1988): 266–78.

5. E. Doverborg, "Forskolebarn Och Matematik? (Preschool Children and Mathematics)," *Publikation fran Institutionen for Pedagogik* Goteborgs Universitet, No. 5 (1987).

6. N. Mikkelson, "Sendak, Snow White, and the Child as a Literary Critic," *Language Arts* 62, no. 4 (1985): 362–73.

7. S. Kontos, "Adult-Child Interaction and the Origins of Metacognition," *Journal of Educational Research* 77 (1983): 43–54.

8. E. Metz (Achilles), "Movement as a Musical Response Among Preschool Children," *Journal of Research in Music Education* 47, no. 1 (1989): 48–60.

9. S. M. Ervin, "Imitation and Structural Change in Children's Language" In *New Directions in the Study of Language*, ed. E. H. Lenneberg (Cambridge, MA: MIT Press, 1964).

10. I. Bretherton, S. McNew, and M. Beeghley-Smith, "Early Person Knowledge as Expressed in Gestural and Verbal Communication: When Do Infants Acquire a 'Theory of Mind'?" in *Infant Social Cognition*, ed. M. E. Lamb and L. R. Sherrod (Hillsdale, NJ: Lawrence Erlbaum Associates, 1981).

11. R. Marzano, et al. *Dimensions of Thinking* (Alexandria, VA: The Association for Supervision and Curriculum Development, 1988), 17.

12. R. Ennis, "Goals for a Critical Thinking Curriculum," in *Developing Minds: A Resource Book for Teaching Thinking*, ed. A. Costa (Alexandria, VA: Association for Supervision and Curriculum Development, 1985).

13. Pogonowski, "Developing Skills"; and Pogonowski, "Critical Thinking."

14. D. Perkins, "Creativity by Design," *Educational Leadership*, 42 (1984): 18–25.

15. D. Halpern, *Thought and Knowledge: An Introduction to Critical Thinking* (Hillsdale, NJ: Erlbaum, 1984).

16. P. Torrance, "Can We Teach Children to Think Creatively?" *Journal of Creative Behavior* 10 (1973): 27–34.

17. B. Martin, *The Implementation of Strategies to Improve the Creative Behaviors of Prospective Preschool Teachers* Practicum Report, Nova University, 1985.

18. B. Andress, *Music Experiences in Early Childhood* (New York: Holt, Rinehart, and Winston, 1980).

19. R. Hess and V. Shipman, "Early Experience and the Socialization of Cognitive Modes in Children," *Child Development* 36 (1965): 869–86; T. McDevitt and R. Hess, *Children's Beliefs as a Route of Influence Between Mother's Direct Control Techniques and Children's Achievement in Mathematics*," Paper presented at the Biennial Conference of the Society for Research in Child Development, Toronto, 1985.

20. J. Eccles, "Expectancies, Values, and Academic Behaviors." In J. Spence, ed. *Achievement and Achievement Motives: Psychosocial and Social Approaches* (New York: Freeman, 1983).

21. N. Chavkin and D. Williams, "Critical Issues in Teacher Training for Parent Involvement," *Educational Horizons* 66 (1988): 87–89.

22. A. Nevin, J. Thousand, P. Paolucci-Whitcomb, and R. Villa, "Collaborative Consultation: Empowering Public School Personnel to Provide Heterogenous Schooling for All—Or Who Rang That Bell?" *Journal of Educational and Psychosocial Consultation* 1, no. 1 (1990): 41–99.

23. D. Elkind, "Hurried Children—Stressed Children," in *The Young Child and Music: Contemporary Principles in Child Development and Music Education*, ed. J. Boswell (Reston, VA: Music Educators National Conference, 1985).

24. L. Katz, "Dispositions in Early Childhood Education," *ERIC/EECE Bulletin* 18 (1985): 2.

Elayne Achilles is assistant professor of education at Arizona State University, West Campus, and is a licensed instructor of Dalcroze Eurhythmics. Her research focuses on movement as a musical response among preschool children, a topic that she has presented at many national and regional conferences and clinics.

"Should young children be exposed to a variety of multicultural songs, finger plays, instruments, and sounds in both a structured and play environment? If so, how can a meaningful multicultural program be developed that involves more than a 'tourist' or cursory approach to music?" Ellen McCullough-Brabson explores answers to these questions from the viewpoint of the early childhood classroom teacher, which includes the anti-bias perspective, and through the music educator's approach. She shares specific teaching strategies and ethnic music examples and discusses their placement at a developmentally appropriate level. She also provides many practical suggestions for a meaningful multicultural music education curriculum, one that helps young children understand and value cultural diversity.

Early Childhood
Multicultural Music Education

BY ELLEN MCCULLOUGH-BRABSON

erhaps you are familiar with the Indian story about the blind men and the elephant. There were seven blind men who wanted to touch an elephant in order to better understand what an elephant is. They walked to the nearest city to place their hands on the rajah's elephant. Each blind man felt a different part of the animal and concluded it was an object with which he was already familiar. The trunk was like a snake, the body like a wall, the leg like a tree, the ear like a fan, the tail like a rope, and the tusk like a spear. They argued with each other. Which blind man had the correct perception? Curious about the disruption, the rajah appeared and explained that each viewpoint was, indeed, partly correct. When all opinions were considered, there was a clearer understanding of what an elephant really is. In this story, exclusive viewpoints did not work. The blind men comprehended only when they pooled their knowledge and thought inclusively.

A parallel between the story of the blind men and the elephant and the philosophy of early childhood music programs should be drawn. Are our children seeing only the "trunk" of early childhood music, or are we exposing them to the entire "elephant" of music from around the world? Do we present music inclusively or exclusively? Do we have a monocultural or a multicultural viewpoint? Should young children be exposed to a variety of multicultural songs, finger plays, instruments, and sounds in both a structured and play environment? If so, how can a meaningful multicultural program be developed that involves more than a "tourist" or cursory approach to music?

A review of music education literature gives strong support for the design, development, and implementation of multicultural music education programs. Although the importance of the use of multicultural music materials for early childhood programs is seldom directly addressed, the rationale given for musical inclusiveness for other age brackets is quite applicable to early childhood. It is very difficult, if not impossible, to understand "elephantness" or the totality of music, unless you have been exposed to all of the "limbs."

Multicultural Rationale

Recent studies of multicultural music dispute the idea that the United States is a melting pot.

There are numerous groups in our country that have retained their own identity yet have contributed richly to a heterogeneous whole. More accurate analogies describing the population have been used. Perhaps a "tossed salad" or "cultural mosaic" comparison is more realistic. Like a tossed salad, each ingredient keeps its identity while contributing to the whole.

The implication for music is obvious. What is American music? Is it music based on Western European tradition? Is it African-American music? Is it Hispanic music? Is it music from an Asian musical tradition? Is American Indian music the "true" American music? Or is it music based on yet another cultural tradition? Robert Garfias, ethnomusicologist, addressed this issue:

> By allowing the specifics to define the whole, we as Americans have, in large measure, been taught to view the American culture as one homogeneous tradition. Upon reflection, we all realize that there are a number of different cultures that we consider American. . . . In many, music may be the culture's strongest or most widely perceived manifestation.[1]

Is it essential that music educators take an inclusive viewpoint regarding the types of music used in early childhood programs?

A frequently heard but much disputed statement is, "music is the universal language of mankind." The use of "language" in this sentence implies an immediacy of understanding. However, anyone listening to a *gamelan, gagaku,* or *didjeridoo* for the first time is hard-pressed to explain what he or she heard. Study and exposure are required to understand world musics. Nonetheless, an emotional response may be triggered on the first hearing. Perhaps a more accurate statement would be, "music is the universal response of humankind."

There are countless ways to make music. These varied musical systems have been described as equally logical but different. In fact, ethnomusicologists and music educators have described music as a world phenomenon.[2] An elitist viewpoint that designates one type of music as "best" can certainly be challenged.

Proponents of multicultural music education believe that exposure to many different types of music helps children of all ages to develop polymusicality or flexibility in their musical response, thinking, and judgment. Anderson and Campbell state, "Research has shown that when students gain a positive attitude toward one `foreign' music and are able to perform and listen intelligently to that music, they become more flexible in their attitudes toward other unfamiliar musics."[3] When hearing new music, children are encouraged to say, "I don't understand that," rather than, "I don't like that."

World music should also be studied for its own intrinsic worth and value. The common elements of music are often used as a starting point. How does the music of another culture use rhythm, melody, form, harmony, tone color, and dynamics? Indeed, can all musical cultures be analyzed by these parameters? Although the prekindergarten-age child will not be able to examine the common elements at a highly sophisticated level, basic contrasts in sound such as loud/soft, high/low, long/short, and fast/slow can be identified.

Demographic predictions alone provide a powerful rationale for the inclusion of multicultural music education in the early childhood curriculum. By the end of the twenty-first century, the majority cultures of the United States will be a minority. The implications are obvious. An exclusive viewpoint that exposes children to only one type of music will ignore the cultural make-up of most of our society.

The most compelling argument for multicultural music in early childhood programs is the fact that exposure to a wide variety of music can promote and develop children's understanding, tolerance, respect, and sensitivity toward other cultures. Can a multicultural music curriculum help preschoolers live in a culturally diverse world? Gable suggests, "Not only can students deepen their own cultural identities through the study of world musics, but they can gain a better understanding of the identities of other students as well. This will lead, in turn, to a greater tolerance and respect for values and beliefs of all peoples, which should be a major goal of education."[4] We live in a rich, colorful, and exciting world in which differences contribute significantly to the whole. Exposure to different types of music in early childhood programs helps prekindergartners understand the music and people of other cultures. And, most important, it can help young children develop skills to cope better in a diverse world.

Early Childhood Multicultural Rationale

Music educators are not alone in their support for a multicultural curriculum. Early childhood specialists also have rallied around the concept that we live in a culturally diverse world that should be reflected in the prekindergarten environment. To present only one cultural perspective in an early childhood program is inaccurate and may even adversely affect the child's development of racial awareness and attitudes.[5] Kendall justified the inclusion of multiculturalism in early childhood programs by the following:

> Multicultural education has five primary goals: first, to teach children to respect others' cultures and values as well as their own; second, to help all children learn to function successfully in a multicultural, multiracial society; third, to develop a positive self-concept in those children who are most affected by racism—children of color; fourth, to help all children experience both their differences as culturally diverse people and their similarities as human beings in positive ways; and fifth, to encourage children to experience people of diverse cultures working together as unique parts of a whole community.[6]

Multicultural proponents from both the music education and early childhood professions assert that an inclusive viewpoint of our world is imperative.

In spite of the persuasive arguments for multicultural early childhood programs, skeptics have questioned the focus on cultural diversity. They contend that prekindergarten children are color-blind and unaware of differences. But studies provide convincing evidence that young children are, indeed, cognizant of differences in race and color by the age of three or four. In fact, children begin to develop positive and negative feelings regarding color at the same time.[7] Phyllis A. Katz, early childhood researcher and educator, addressed this issue and cautioned that "the tree grows as the twig is bent."[8] Although there is no conclusive evidence as to what causes the "twig to bend," influencing factors may be attitudes reflected by parents, society, care-givers, and even positive and negative word associations. It is easier to "bend the twig" in the "right" direction while it is still a twig than to uproot a mature tree of prejudice.

What can be done to foster positive attitudes and awareness? Programs that affirm difference are a good starting point and multicultural music is a lively and creative first step.

One early childhood plan that confronts cultural diversity head-on is called the anti-bias curriculum. Derman-Sparks states:

> Anti-bias curriculum embraces an educational philosophy as well as specific techniques and content. It is value based: Differences are good, oppressive ideas and behaviors are not. It sets up a creative tension between respecting differences

and not accepting unfair beliefs and acts. It asks teachers and children to confront troublesome issues rather than covering them up. An anti-bias perspective is integral to all aspects of daily classroom life. [9]

An important component of the anti-bias curriculum is the development of empowerment within each child so that the child can recognize bias and injustice and react with a creative and powerful response.

Proponents of the anti-bias curriculum believe that although multicultural programs designed for prekindergarten are sincere in their message, they can also deteriorate into a "tourist curriculum." A tourist curriculum is one where only special holidays of selected cultures are celebrated and then the cultural groups are neglected the rest of the year. Or one in which singing one song of another cultural group is supposed to represent the entire culture. Trivializing, tokenism, disconnecting cultural diversity from daily classroom life, stereotyping, and misrepresentation are all possible side effects of a tourist curriculum. [10]

Although warnings about the effects of a tourist curriculum have some validity, music educators should not be intimidated or disheartened. As the Chinese proverb says, a thousand mile journey begins with the first step. Music educators should be encouraged to use the music of selected cultural celebrations or songs of various ethnic groups as a starting point in the development of a multicultural curriculum. As the teacher becomes more familiar with the music of other cultural groups, the program can continually expand until it is integrated into the daily music preschool plan. What, then, are practical guidelines and strategies that should be taken into consideration when planning a meaningful early childhood program?

Multicultural Music Guidelines for Early Childhood Programs

Several guidelines need to be examined before a multicultural music program for preschoolers is implemented. Issues that should be addressed include: the development of cultural sensitivity, the investigation of authenticity, the breadth and depth of the multicultural music materials, the relationship of music to the total curriculum, the creative use of resources, and the characteristics of prekindergartner's development.

Cultural sensitivity. Many early childhood educators no longer sing "Ten Little Indians" with their preschoolers because it implies that all American Indians look alike. For a similar reason, some prekindergarten specialists ask their children to sit "pretzel-style" rather than in a stereotyped "Indian-style" position. And there are sensitive teachers who carefully screen all song lyrics and figures of speech that might contain offensive language about cultural groups. For example, the popular early childhood song "Taffy" has been identified as music with questionable lyrics. The words are, "Taffy was a Welshman. Taffy was a thief. Taffy came to our house and stole a roast of beef." A negative stereotype is projected. Although some may protest that these examples are not worth arguing about, multicultural advocates would counter that they are illustrations of teachers who have shown cultural sensitivity. Music educators should do the same.

Cultural sensitivity includes knowledge of cultural group names. Would a white child prefer to be labeled as White or Anglo-American? Would a Black child select to be called Black or African-American? Are Hispanic children referred to as Hispanic, Spanish, Mexican, or Chicano? Is American Indian or Native American the more appropriate term? Although many preschoolers may not know the preferential name of their race, parents can supply that information. In fact, the answers might change from time to time depending on the audience and even from child to child.

Because a child's self-worth and self-esteem are greatly influenced by his or her teacher's attitudes, music educators must exhibit cultural sensitivity toward each child. The results are bound to be positive. Although there are many issues regarding the development of cultural sensitivity, awareness on the part of the music educator is an important starting point.

Authenticity. According to the dictionary, authenticity means the quality of being authoritative, valid, true, real, or genuine. Although a definition for the word is easily found, the issue of authenticity becomes more complex when examining music. What is authentic music of a culture? What criterion is used when judging the authenticity of a piece of music? And what makes a piece of music unauthentic? For the purpose of this discussion, authentic music is music that is considered to be a valid representation of a cultural group. Music educators should ask the following questions when deciding whether or not a musical selection is authentic.

Is the music performed in the native language? Because language is an integral component of culture and an important part of an individual's identity, the use of the native tongue in songs and listening examples is recommended. Preschoolers are quite responsive to listening to and speaking in different languages and should be given the opportunity to do so. An accurate translation of the words is essential. Children will be curious to know what the song means.

Is information regarding the cultural context given? For example, if a song is described as a "game from Ghana," data regarding the circumstances in which the game is played, whether or not both boys and girls play the game, and other pertinent information should be included. Music is integrated with life. The cultural context of music can provide a wealth of information that can promote a child's understanding of another culture.

A third question to consider is whether the style of the song and its accompaniment are appropriate. Should a Navajo song be sung in the traditional singing style? If there is a piano accompaniment to a Navajo song, would it be considered authentic? Many excellent recordings are available that highlight the appropriate style and accompaniment of music from a wide variety of cultures. These recordings enable teachers to bring the music of another culture into the classroom in a meaningful way.

Music educators must use their best professional judgement and integrity when evaluating multicultural music materials for use in early childhood programs. Although there are many excellent materials available that are considered to be authentic, there are also other sources that should be red-flagged.

Breadth and depth. A multicultural music program should have both breadth and depth in order to avoid a "tourist" approach. Music from a wide variety of cultures supplies breadth; a significant amount of material that represents each culture gives depth. However, as stated earlier, music educators may have to start with a few selected materials and then gradually expand their repertoire. It is unrealistic to expect a music teacher to become an expert on each musical culture overnight. Nonetheless, music educators who are truly interested in developing a meaningful music curriculum for prekindergartners must start somewhere and should be encouraged to attend teacher in-service conferences, workshops, and university classes to develop their curriculum materials.

Integration. Music should not be an isolated part of the program. For example, the physical environment of the preschool setting is an excellent forum that can be used to reflect cultural diversity. Pictures of musicians and musical instruments from around the world should be prominently displayed. However, to avoid a tourist approach, it is recommended that musicians be shown in both traditional and contemporary dress. It is important to display pictures of people from other cultures that reflect daily life, not just celebrations or pictures from the past.[11] Music educators should also integrate music centers into the physical setting so that prekindergartners have the opportunity to play freely with multicultural music materials through spontaneous singing, listening, playing instruments, moving, and creating. Specific suggestions for creating music centers are presented on page 88.

In order for music teachers to begin to understand a culture and how music is integrated into the life of other people, study of the geography, history, economy, literature, politics, social structure, and related arts of the culture is beneficial. Although much of the information gleaned from this scrutiny would be far too complex to share with young children, it increases the music educator's perception of how other people live, think, work, dress, worship, play, and express their feelings through the arts.

Resources. A wealth of resources is available to the music educator to enrich a multicultural music curriculum. The best place to start is with the child. Many preschoolers will know finger plays, rhymes, and songs that their parents have performed with them at home. An attentive teacher can encourage a child to share his or her musical experiences with other children. Parents are also excellent resources and may agree to perform the music from their culture for the class. Community members may be willing to act as guest artists or music informants. Universities, colleges, libraries, and similar sources should be searched for multicultural enrichment programs. Indeed, some of the best resources are found in your own backyard.

Developmental characteristics. A look at the developmental characteristics of the prekindergarten child is crucial when planning a multicultural music program. Music educators should carefully examine several of the many publications that specifically address how young children behave, think, and learn. This will provide the framework for selecting age-appropriate activities. Andress cautions that well-intentioned music educators often "extend the existing music program downward," which may result in inappropriate activities for the prekindergarten child. [12]

Music educators need to ask several questions when planning musical experiences for preschoolers. How do young children learn? Is the child developmentally ready for this activity? What musical elements can a preschooler conceptualize? When should a music teacher label a musical concept? Is the musical experience child-oriented? Although many more questions could be asked, music educators need to be sensitive to the requirement for age-appropriate activities for preschoolers.

The importance of play in musical learning is a developmental characteristic of the young child that should be highlighted. Early childhood experts contend that much significant musical learning takes place during the child's spontaneous musical play. Indeed, the impact of play on the child's understanding of the world has been well-documented. Music educators will need to take this information into account and devise a curriculum in which children can play freely with multicultural music materials. Specific strategies for doing this are presented in the next section of this chapter.

Another preschooler developmental characteristic that should be considered is music preference. According to Scott, "Research in music preference in preschoolers shows that they are open to all kinds of music and have not yet begun to form strong preferences." [13] The implications for early childhood multicultural music programs are exciting. If prekindergartners are receptive to all types of music, what better time than early childhood to introduce them to a wide variety of world musics?

Developing cultural sensitivity, investigating authenticity, exploring both the breadth and depth of the curriculum, integrating music into the program, utilizing a variety of resources, and examining developmental characteristics of the young child are all components that should be addressed in the planning stages of a multicultural music curriculum. Once these six guidelines have been considered, specific teaching strategies can be developed.

2. La gallina (the hen)—clo, clo, clo!
3. El cochito (little pig)—oink-oink!
4. El perrito (little dog)—woof, woof, woof!
5. El toro (the bull)—moooooo!

Translation
Come to my farm my friend.
Come to my farm my friend.
The little chicken sounds like this, pio, pio.
The little chicken sounds like this, pio, pio.
Go my friend, go my friend, go, go, go.
Go my friend, go my friend, go, go, go.

Figure 1. "Mi Chacra"
Cantemos Records, P.O. Box 246, San Cristobal, New Mexico 87564.
Used by permission. Adapted by Jenny Vincent.

Specific Teaching Strategies

Traditionally, early childhood music programs were taught by a music educator who sang songs, chanted rhymes, and performed finger plays with children during a time set aside for group activity. Perhaps at this time a simple singing game would be taught or a musical instrument introduced for the children to pass around, play, and explore. Although this kind of teacher-directed activity is an important part of the prekindergarten program, another equally valuable music experience is that of child-initiated musical play. Both teacher-directed and child-initiated musical activities must be considered when planning a multicultural program.

Singing, chanting, playing instruments, and moving and listening to music are the typical skills children experience during the teacher-directed part of the early childhood music pro-

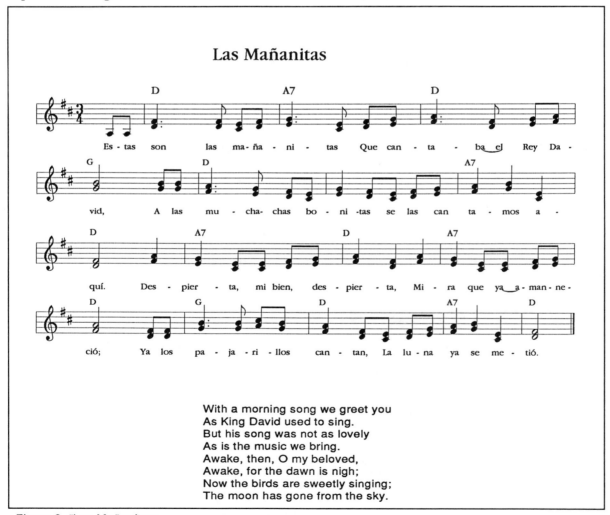

Las Mañanitas

Es - tas son las ma - ña - ni - tas Que can - ta - ba el Rey Da -
vid, A las mu - cha - chas bo - ni -tas se las can - ta - mos a -
quí. Des - pier - ta, mi bien, des - pier - ta, Mi - ra que ya a - man - ne -
ció; Ya los pa - ja - ri - llos can - tan, La lu - na ya se me - tió.

With a morning song we greet you
As King David used to sing.
But his song was not as lovely
As is the music we bring.
Awake, then, O my beloved,
Awake, for the dawn is nigh;
Now the birds are sweetly singing;
The moon has gone from the sky.

Figure 2. "Las Mañanitas:
English translation by Janet E. Tobitt, Olcutt Sanders, and Phyllis Sanders.
"Las Mañanitas" from Amigos Cantando.
Copyright © 1948, World Around Songs, Inc. Copyright renewed. Used with permission.

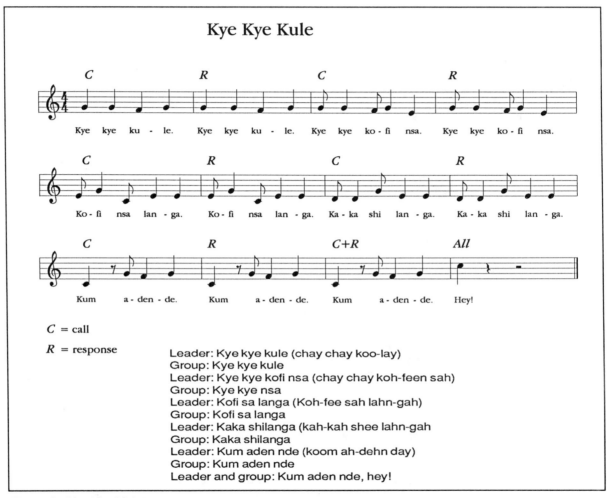

Figure 3. "Kye Kye Kule"

This is a very popular motion game played by young children in Ghana. It is even found in other parts of Africa with very similar words that may come from a mixture of dialects, but have not been pinpointed as part of a particular language and do not convey any specific meaning.

Edna Smith Edet includes a Nigerian version of "Kye Kye Kule" in *The Griot Sings: Songs from the Black World*. The words are: "Che Che kule, Oku salala; He malila, ho." She notes, "On 'ho' the leader chooses a successor."

"Kye Kye Kule" is suitable for use with preschool or older children. The leader sings the first phrase, simultaneously patting his or her head four times on the beat. The group responds by repeating the phrase and

the motion. Next, the leader sings the second phrase while tapping his or her shoulders four times and twisting the upper torso from side to side as well. Again, the group repeats the phrase and the motion. Next hands go to waist, the twisting continues in an animated way, and the group follows. Next the leader taps the knees and the group copies. Lastly, the leader bends over to touch ankles on "kum" and touch waist on "adende." The group responds and then leader and group touch ankles and waist in unison, then all throw hands over their head and shout "Hey!"

Students take turns being the leader. Add a little spice by creating a small percussion ensemble to accompany the group.

From *Let Your Voice Be Heard! Songs from Ghana and Zimbabwe* by Abraham Kobena Adzinyah, Dumisani Maraire, and Judith Cook Tucker. ©1986, published by World Music Press, P.O. Box 2565, Danbury, CT 06813. Used by permission.

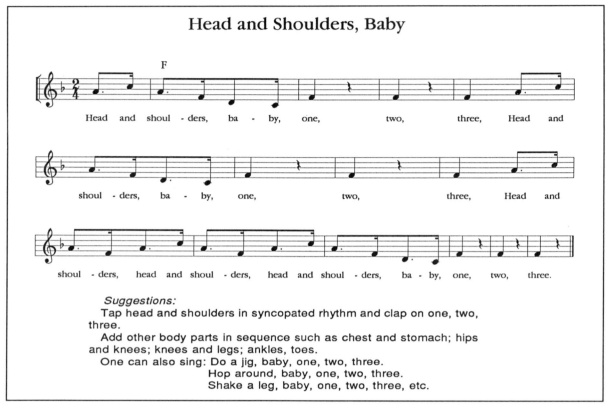

Head and Shoulders, Baby

Head and shoul - ders, ba - by, one, two, three, Head and

shoul - ders, ba - by, one, two, three, Head and

shoul - ders, head and shoul - ders, head and shoul - ders, ba - by, one, two, three.

Suggestions:
Tap head and shoulders in syncopated rhythm and clap on one, two, three.
Add other body parts in sequence such as chest and stomach; hips and knees; knees and legs; ankles, toes.
One can also sing: Do a jig, baby, one, two, three.
Hop around, baby, one, two, three.
Shake a leg, baby, one, two, three, etc.

Figure 4.
Reprinted with the permission of Merrill, an imprint of Macmillan Publishing Company, from Music: A Way of Life for the Young Child, 4th ed., by Kathleen M. Bayless and Marjorie E. Ramsey. Copyright © 1991 by Macmillan Publishing Company.

gram. A multicultural music curriculum can be easily integrated into the existing structure. Instead of using music from one culture, songs, chants, finger plays, dances, listening excerpts, and musical instruments from a variety of cultures can be combined with materials the teacher already uses and knows well. As mentioned earlier, a starting point for the development of multicultural materials may be using the music from the holidays or celebrations of selected ethnic groups. Or perhaps the music educator will choose to explore the music of one unfamiliar culture for the entire year. As the teacher develops a wider repertoire of materials, the multicultural music program will steadily grow until it is, indeed, multidimensional.

Children's songs collected from a variety of cultures could be another first step in developing multicultural materials. These songs could be categorized into song types such as lullabies, work songs, action songs, fun songs, birthday and special day songs, circle game songs, animal songs, or songs that describe body parts. The list is extensive. These songs should then be integrated into the daily music program. For example, when singing "Old MacDonald," why not sing the Spanish version of "Mi Chacra" too? (See figure 1.) Or when celebrating a child's birthday, have the children sing "Las Mañanitas" as well as "Happy Birthday." (See figure 2.) Illustrations of children's songs from around the world are given in figures 3–6.

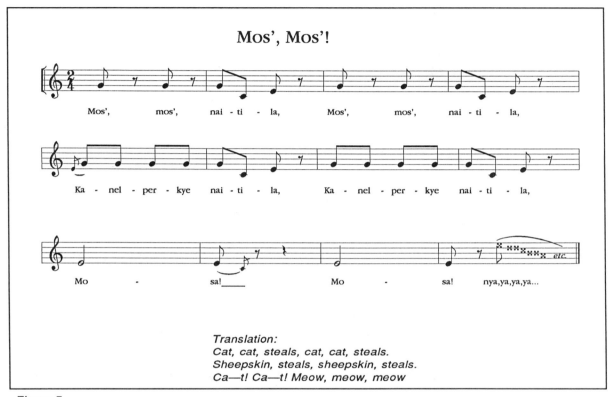

Mos', Mos'!

Translation:
Cat, cat, steals, cat, cat, steals.
Sheepskin, steals, sheepskin, steals.
Ca—t! Ca—t! Meow, meow, meow

Figure 5.
From Multicultural Perspectives in Music Education, *edited by William M. Anderson and Patricia Shehan Campbell (Reston, VA: Music Educators National Conference, 1989), 37. Song collected by David McAllester.*

If the music is too difficult, the teacher could sing the song for the students. A "goosebump" listening experience for the child could be the result. For example, the children could sing the response "Um-hm" while the teacher sings the verses to the Anglo-American ballad, "Mr. Frog Went A-Courtin'." Or the teacher could sing "Sakura," a traditional Japanese song that describes cherry blossoms, and have the children just listen.

There is a wealth of children's songs from each culture. One delightful song type that may be unfamiliar to American music educators is a genre of Japanese songs in which the child draws one part of a picture for each phrase of the song. At the conclusion of

the song the drawing is complete. (See Figure 7.)

Daily experiences with multicultural songs, finger plays and nursery rhymes, as well as listening examples, instruments, and dances will provide children with a broader perspective of how other cultural groups express feelings through sound. Whether done in a teacher-directed group activity or as a teacher-initiated, one-on-one experience with an individual child, multicultural music materials can contribute richly to the early childhood curriculum.

Although teacher-directed activities are certainly very important, the child's natural sense of exploration through play should also be nurtured in a multicultural music environment. An

Ninni Baba

Nin - ni Ba - ba Ni - ni____ mak-han ro - ti chi - ni

Me - ra bhay-ya khan-na man-ge dar-mi ke do ser.

Translation:
Come now, Sleep, and bring here candy for my small one;
Or perhaps he'd like some butter, Thinking it is all fun.

Figure 6.
English translation by Katherine F. Rohrbough.
From Joyful Songs of India *(Delaware, OH: Cooperative Recreation Service, Inc., 1956), 16. Used by permission.*

A Be Ce
el alfabeto

A be ce che de e ef - fe ge____ ha - che

i jo - ta ka e - le e - lle e - me e - ne e - ñe

oh pe cu e - re e - rre e - se te u ve y do - ble

oo e - quis y y - grie - ga con ze - ta ya a - ca - bé.

Translation:
A B C Ch D E F G H
I J K L Ll M N Ñ
O P Q R Rr S T U V and W
X and Y with Z. Now I'm done.

Figure 7.
Cantemos Records, P.O. Box 246, San Cristobal, New Mexico 87564.
Used by permission. Adapted by Jenny Vincent.

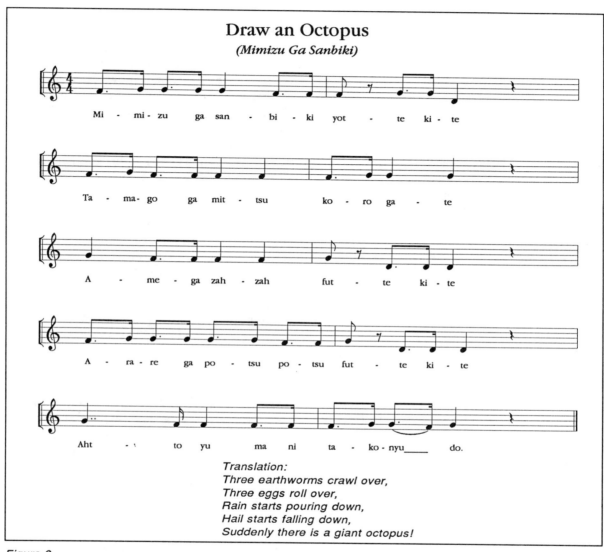

Draw an Octopus
(*Mimizu Ga Sanbiki*)

Translation:
*Three earthworms crawl over,
Three eggs roll over,
Rain starts pouring down,
Hail starts falling down,
Suddenly there is a giant octopus!*

Figure 8.

Translated by Reiko Niiy-Tigges.

Directions for drawing game:

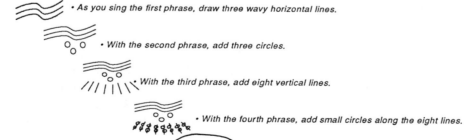

• As you sing the first phrase, draw three wavy horizontal lines.

• With the second phrase, add three circles.

• With the third phrase, add eight vertical lines.

• With the fourth phrase, add small circles along the eight lines.

• While singing the fifth phrase, draw a big circle to make the octopus's face.

Source: Professor Reiko Hata, 4-2-25 Nigawacho, Nshinomiya City 662, Japan. Used by permission.

effective way to do this is to develop music centers that focus on music representative of a wide variety of ethnic groups. A music center is a designated area in the room where children can freely explore music through play by creating, listening, moving, playing instruments, and singing as they choose. Kenney states:

> Music centers give children freedom to explore timbre, rhythm, melody, form, and expressive music qualities, as well as singing, playing instruments, composing, listening, categorizing, and evaluating. The teacher creates the environment but does not dictate the learning process. She or he can assist by labeling the results for the children as they produce sounds; for example, "That is a high sound" (loud sound, fast, slow, ringing, or clicking sound). [14]

The music educator's task is to create a stimulating environment in which the child can freely discover and explore music. A multicultural emphasis in music can lead the child to actively experience a wide variety of ethnic music through play. Music centers commonly include areas for singing, moving and listening to music, and playing instruments.

The singing music center should provide opportunities for the child to "play" with multicultural songs. A tape recorder and cassettes that feature a wide variety of ethnic music that the children have sung in group time, as well as new songs, should be included. The child is free to respond to the songs in any way that she or he desires. Pictures placed in the singing center may trigger a child's spontaneous singing of a song that he or she associates with the picture. For example, if the child views a farmyard scene picture, he or she might spontaneously sing "Mi Chacra" or "Old MacDonald." If puppets or dolls are placed in the singing center, children might use them as props to assist them in singing. An illustration is a child's use of a finger puppet to sing the response "yes ma'am" to the Afro-American song "Did You Feed My Cow?" Only songs of excellent quality with distinct, clear melodies and appropriate accompaniment should be used. Children might also use the multicultural music as a springboard to create their own songs.

The listening and moving center should be designed to stimulate the young child to listen to all types of multicultural music as well to perform spontaneous movement in response to the music he or she is hearing. Therefore, the space in the center must be big enough for the child to move freely. It should also contain a tape recorder and tapes of highest quality of world musics. As mentioned earlier, if a child's musical preference is not set, he or she should be quite responsive to a wide variety of sounds. (See the selected discography that accompanies this chapter.)

Another interesting idea, although one that is not directly related to the listening center is what Andress describes as "Play Along the Day." [15] This is an activity in which different types of music are played throughout the day to signal nap time, story time, group time, and other regularly scheduled daily events. Why not use multicultural music for the signals? For example, an Indian raga traditionally performed in the morning could be used as the morning circle-time signal. Or perhaps Japanese *koto* music could be played as an indicator of nap time.

Of all the multicultural music centers designed for children's play, the instrument center is one of the most exciting and intriguing. Children are fascinated with sound. Although it may appear to an adult that the children are banging on an instrument, musical learning may, indeed, be taking place. In fact, a more appropriate name for the instrument center is the "sound exploration center." This area can provide young children with a wonderful opportunity to freely explore a wide variety of instruments from around the world. As the children spontaneously create sounds on ethnic instruments, many musical discoveries can take place. Preschoolers will have the opportunity to experience basic musical concepts such as high and low, loud and soft, long and short, and fast and slow sounds.

Music educators must caution young children to treat all musical instruments with respect so that none will be damaged or destroyed. If budget restraints restrict the purchase of global musical instruments, homemade instruments that stimulate the sound and appearance of the original instrument should be used. Pictures of instruments, keyed to a corresponding tape that illustrates how the instrument is played, should be included in the instrument center. Excellent resources for making musical instruments of other cultures, as well as instruments pictures are available. (See the selected bibliography at the end of this chapter.)

Music educators should also provide musical instrument games and activities for children to play in the instrument center. For example, preschoolers will enjoy matching the sounds of similar and different instruments, performing the maracas to a recording of mariachi music, and playing musical-instrument matching games.

A balance of teacher-directed and child-initiated activities is an important consideration when planning a meaningful multicultural music education curriculum for early childhood programs. Both can richly contribute to a child's understanding of cultural diversity.

Conclusion

An examination of the justifications for a multicultural early childhood program, a discussion of guidelines that should be considered before its implementation, and an overview of specific teaching strategies have been presented. It is up to the music educator to accept, expand, or reject these ideas. Nonetheless, multicultural education advocates have raised some very complex questions. What are the benefits when music educators have an inclusive viewpoint of music

that allows the child to see the whole "elephant" rather than just one "limb"? Can multicultural music education make a positive impact on the life of a preschooler? Does exposure to music nurture a child's understanding, tolerance, respect, and sensitivity toward other cultures? Indeed, can experience with world music help young children to cope in a diverse world? Although the answers to these questions could take a lifetime of reflection and discovery, they need to be addressed.

In his highly acclaimed children's book *People*, Peter Spier discusses the issue of cultural diversity. His colorful, detailed illustrations depict people from all over the world. He emphasizes that all people eat, dress, work, play, celebrate, dance, and create, but not necessarily in the same ways. Spier concludes that the fact that each person is totally unique and unlike any person who has ever lived before is a spectacular phenomenon. It is our differences that richly contribute to the whole.

Music should be viewed from the same perspective. People from all cultures express feelings and emotions through sound in a wide variety of interesting and dynamic ways. Diversity is what makes music exciting. Early childhood music educators should embrace a multicultural philosophy and think inclusively. Multicultural music is, indeed, a cause for celebration!

Notes

1. R. Garfias, "Music in the United States: Community of Cultures," *Music Educators Journal* 69, no. 9 (1983): 31.
2. W. M. Anderson and P. Shehan Campbell, eds., *Multicultural Perspectives in Music Education* (Reston, VA: Music Educators National Conference, 1989), 3.
3. Anderson and Campbell, *Multicultural Perspectives*, 4.
4. S. Gable, "A Multiculutral Curriculum," *Music Educators Journal* 69, no. 9 (1983): 40.

5. F. E. Kendall, *Diversity in the Classroom: A Multicultural Approach to the Education of Young Children* (New York: Teachers College, Columbia University, 1983), 20.

6. Kendall, *Diversity in the Classroom*, 3.

7. Kendall, *Diversity in the Classroom*, 20.

8. P. A. Katz, "The Acquisition of Racial Attitudes in Children," *Towards the Elimination of Racism* (New York: Pergamon Press Inc., 1976), 125.

9. L. Derman-Sparks and A.B.C. Task Force, *Anti-Bias Curriculum: Tools for Empowering Young Children* (Washington, DC: National Association for the Education of Young Children, 1989).

10. Derman-Sparks, *Anti-Bias Curriculum*, 63.

11. Derman-Sparks, *Anti-Bias Curriculum*, 63.

12. B. Andress, "Music for Every Stage: How Much? What Kind? How Soon?" *Music Educators Journal* 76, no. 2 (1989): 23.

13. C. R. Scott, "How Children Grow—Musically," *Music Educators Journal* 76, no. 2 (1989): 33–34.

14. S. Kenney, "Music Centers: Freedom to Explore," *Music Educators Journal* 76, no. 2 (1989): 33–34.

15. B. Andress, ed., *Music in Early Childhood* (Washington, DC: Music Educators National Conference, 1973), 47.

Resources

Selected Bibliography

Anderson, William M., and Patricia Shehan Campbell. *Multicultural Perspectives in Music Education.* Reston, VA: Music Educators National Conference, 1989.

Anderson, William M. "The Teacher as Translator of Culture." *Music Educators Journal* 69, no. 9 (May 1983): 32.

Andress, Barbara. "Music for Every Stage: How Much? What Kind? How Soon?" *Music Educators Journal* 76, no. 2 (October 1989), 22–27.

Andress, Barbara, ed. *Music in Early Childhood.* Washington, DC: Music Educators National Conference, 1973.

Andress, Barbara, ed. *Promising Practices: Prekindergarten Music Education.* Reston, VA: Music Educators National Conference, 1989.

Ardley, Neil. *Eyewitness Books: Music.* New York: Alfred A. Knopf, 1989.

Botermans, Jack, Herman Dewit, and Hans Goddefroy. *Making and Playing Musical Instruments.* Seattle: University of Washington Press, 1989.

Derman-Sparks, Louise, and the A.B.C. Task Force. *Anti-Bias Curriculum: Tools for Empowering Young Children.* Washington, DC: National Association for the Education of Young Children, 1989.

Diagram Group. *Music Instruments of the World.* New York: Facts on File Publications, 1979.

Fox, Donna Brink. "Music, Development, and the Young Child." *Music Educators Journal* 77, no. 5 (January 1991): 42–46.

Garfias, Robert. "Music in the United States: Community of Cultures." *Music Educators Journal* 69, no. 9 (May 1983): 30–31.

Hawes, Bess Lomax. "Our Cultural Mosaic." *Music Educators Journal* 69, no. 9 (May 1983): 26–27.

Hunter, Ilene, and Marilyn Judson. *Simple Folk Instruments to Make and to Play.* New York: Simon and Schuster, 1977.

Kenney, Susan. "Music Centers: Freedom to Explore." *Music Educators Journal* 76, no. 2 (October 1989): 32–36.

Mayers, Florence Cassen. *ABC Musical Instruments from the Metropolitan Museum of Art.* New York: Harry N. Abrams, 1988.

Pond, Donald. "The Young Child's Playful World of Sound." *Music Educators Journal* 66, no. 7 (March 1980): 39–41.

Ross, Jerrold. *A Framework for Multicultural Arts Education.* New York University: National Arts Education Research Center, 1989.

Saracho, Olivia N., and Bernard Spodek, eds. *Understanding the Multicultural Experience in Early Childhood Education.* Washington, DC: National Association for the Education of Young Children, 1983.

Scott, Carol Rogel. "How Children Grow—Musically." *Music Educators Journal* 76, no. 2 (October 1989): 28–31.

Spier, Peter. *People.* New York: Doubleday, 1980.

Trimillos, Ricardo D. "The Sound of a Bell: Aesthetics and World Music." *Music Educators Journal* 69, no. 6 (May 1983): 44–46.

Selected Discography

African Mbira: Music of the Shona People of Rhodesia. Nonesuch Explorer Series H-72043.

The Appalachian Dulcimer by Jean Ritchie: An Instruction Record. Folkways FI 8352.

Arab Music, Vol. 1. Lyrichord LLST 7186.

Art of the Koto: The Music of Japan Played by Kimia Eto. Elektra Records EKL 234.

Chad (Kanem). *An Anthology of African Music.* UNESCO Collection. Barenreiter Musicaphone BM 30-L2309.

Children's Songs and Games from the Southern Mountains. Folkways FC 7054.

China's Instrumental Heritage. Lyrichord LL92.

Classical Music of India. Nonesuch Explorer Series H-72014.

Cloud Dance Songs of San Juan Pueblo. Indian House (Box 472, Taos, NM 87571).

Flute Songs of the Kiowa and Comanche. Indian House (Box 472, Taos, NM 87571).

Folk Music of the United States from the Archive of Folk Song, Navajo. Library of Congress AAFS L41.

Golden Rain: Balinese Gamelan Music. Nonesuch Explorer Series H-72028.

Hawaiian Chant, Hula, and Music. Folkways FW 8750.

Kingdom of the Sun, Peru's Inca Heritage. Nonesuch Explorer Series H-72029.

Music from the Heart of Africa: Burundi. Nonesuch Explorer Series H-72057.

Music of Southeast Asia. Folkways FE 4428.

Music of the Dan. Barenreiter Musicaphone BM 30-L2301.

Old Mother Hippletoe: Rural and Urban Children's Songs. New World Records 245.

Sounds of India: Ravi Shanker. Columbia LS 9296.

Step It Down. Rounder Records 8804.

Traditional Folk Songs of Japan. Folkways FE 4534.

Traditional Music of Peru. Folkways FE 4456.

Ellen McCullough-Brabson is associate professor of music education at the University of New Mexico. She has served as a K–6 general music specialist in the Cincinnati and Tucson Sunnyside Public School Districts. She has presented numerous multicultural workshops internationally and nationally, and has published articles on topics including Appalachian music, the dulcimer, and musical instruments from around the world.

Children at risk. Who are they? How can the music educator best guide the at-risk learner? Betty Welsbacher shares a definition that classifies these children into those of established risk, biological risk, and environmental risk. Insight as to how these children are viewed by those in special education, medicine, psychology, and speech pathology are cited. The style of this piece alternates between glimpses into a group of at-risk children in a music classroom setting and comments as to their behavioral responses, and the subsequent planned actions of the teacher.

Meeting Needs

Music Education Experiences of Prekindergarten Children At Risk

BY BETTY WELSBACHER

 am scrunched into a corner near the window, between a pail of sudsy water and the green "blackboard," trying to video-tape everything as the children come tumbling back into the classroom. They have gone for a little walk (to let off energy), all twelve of them, with their teacher and two aides before their special music teacher guides them through some activities we've devised as part of a curricular development module. These formal, academic words seem archaic and out-of-place in the actuality of this lively, spirited group of three- to four-year-olds.

Comfortable and secure in their familiar routine, each child finds a thick carpet square, flops or drops or squiggles onto it, and looks expectantly at the teacher seated on a low stool in their midst. The children are a motley, diverse mixture; they are suspected of having physical, neurological, emotional, or environmental problems and disorders—known and unknown, identified and unidentified. It is possible, or likely, that they may have developmental delays in the future involving areas of motor, language, and cognitive growth, among others. Many are products of low socioeconomic status. All are "at-risk" children. The class is held in a former elementary school in this metropolitan area, which has been transformed into an Early Childhood Center. All students in this school are considered to be high-risk children.

This school uses a more comprehensive interpretation of the terms "at risk" and "high risk" than that endorsed by many service professionals. The writings of education and special education, medicine, psychology, and speech pathology contain these terms more and more frequently, and each discipline intends its own meaning. In fact, the most controversial issue surrounding these children may be what to call them. As always happens with such labels, they vary from coast to coast and from county to county; check your local board of education for the latest acronym. I've chosen to use "at risk" simply because the words describe the problem, not the child.

But many caregivers and professionals now are finding commonality in a definition such as "those infants and very young children who have been exposed to any one of a number of medical factors that may contribute to later developmental delay."[1] Children known to have characteristics that clearly predict developmental delay, such as Down's syndrome, and other recognizable exceptionality categories are not included as part of the high-risk population according to this definition.

A different form of the "at risk" designation for young children adopts this three-item classification: 1. Those of established risk, 2. Those at biological risk, 3. Those at environmental risk.[2]

In this grouping, children of *established risk* are seen as those who are already associated with identified exceptionalities: physical impairment, mental retardation, sensory deficits, neurological dysfunctions—the disabilities that make up the category of special education, including early childhood handicapped (ECH). They are included as being at risk because, at very young ages, the identified exceptionalities do not always become apparent; the four-month-old infant who has not yet been "identified" as having cerebral palsy, for example, may also be a low birth weight baby (LBW), or be the product of an environment that puts him or her at risk from fetal alcohol syndrome or lack of sensory stimulation. The range of identification for known exceptionalities varies greatly: Down's syndrome is usually identified within a year, but generalized mental retardation has a range of up to six years for recognition. Autistic children frequently show few if any characteristic signs until after about eighteen months or older; the onset of autism frequently coincides with the normal period for instigating and expanding spoken language. Further, many children at established risk for exceptionalities deriving from developmental pathology are not routinely classified and identified through medical assessment. For example, only 4.5 percent of children's problems overall are identified at birth by physicians; less than 30 percent are identified before the age of five years. Physicians are more likely to identify less common, more severe problems; only 15 to 25 percent of children with speech and communication impairments, emotional disorders, hyperkinesis (hyperactivity), learning disabilities, and other developmental pathological problems are identified by medical doctors.[3]

This is not a criticism: these latter disabilities only become known, in far more cases than not, when the child begins to need the skills that are lacking or delayed as he or she reaches that developmental level where those skills normally come into play. And many of these developmentally driven disabilities simply are not in the province of the medical doctor: they are only recognized by the child's behavior at a particular developmental level, and then by specialists in nonmedical fields: education, speech pathology, developmental and child psychology, and by special educators or therapists in music and fine arts who teach and work with special learners.

Biological risk implies that no clear abnormality is detected immediately. Examples of factors putting children at biological risk include pregnancy complications—injury, disease, infections, and so on; maternal dysfunctions, such as diabetes; labor complications; infections of the nervous system, as with encephalitis; the ingestion of toxic substances; prematurity; and low birth weight (LBW). Low birth weight is strongly associated with infant death rates; very low birth weight puts a child at serious risk of disability. A premature LBW infant is ten times more likely to be mentally retarded than a normal baby.

Children at *environmental risk* are biologically and genetically intact and normal at birth, but are threatened by their environment. The quality and quantity of maternal and medical care; the opportunity or lack of it for social, educational and sensory stimulation; the presence of a healthy psychological environment; all these and more can be determinants of possible developmental delays.

In the early childhood center I am visiting, there are four different kinds of classes: Head Start, Chapter I, Even Start (all federal or state programs) and Early Childhood Handicapped the most recent (at this writing) "official" category in special education. The children with whom I am waiting for music are, indeed, at-risk children in the letter as well as the spirit of current definitions. They demonstrate many of the same behaviors as do children with traditional etiologies—neurologically damaged, mentally retarded, behavior disordered, physically impaired—but they fall "in the cracks" so far as easy comprehension of their strengths, weaknesses, needs, and preferences are concerned. No clear abnormality has been detected.

At-Risk Children in the Classroom

The children are all settled now; they have looked me over and dismissed me. The video camera is more distracting, but they take it in stride. What they are really interested in is the person who is going to make music with them. To their delight the class begins.

I watch and listen. The children are alert and responsible. They seem comfortable and eager, and obviously enjoy the whole musical experience. But somehow, the behavior of the children in this class looks a little different from that of other such groups I've observed—in subtle ways.

A similar group of children who are not at risk might explore the resources of music and material centers. They might choose and discard objects to play on or with, or to touch. They might sing, sometimes snatches of learned songs, more often their own songs and sing-songs, chanting and singing intermittently, intent on their own agendas. They would, perhaps, pair off briefly, share or exchange instruments or activities, or they might work for some time entirely alone. Music circles and organized play might be favorites of some of the children, but others would come and go in the group,

still preferring more personal games and music.

This real class of at-risk children, however, is engaged in more structured musical experiences. A dozen children are involved in the same activities at the same time. They show few signs of fatigue, disinterest, or hyperactivity. During parts of the class everyone in the circle, individually, has an opportunity to do something alone. One at a time they sing a response; touch hearts on a chart outlining a melody—an ostinato—that they are hearing or singing; jump from heart to heart on the same chart transferred to the floor, setting the tempo with the rate and style of their jumping. Everyone does all these things; more remarkably, each waits his or her turn, and enjoys watching the others take their turns.

Another difference from the hypothetical "normal" group lies in the language level of the at-risk children. There is less chatter here, less exploratory speech or just "trying out" sounds. The language that we do hear is more typical of children just beginning to talk. There are few interjections and comments from the group; they listen more than they speak. One or two children are talking, it would seem, to themselves. But mostly, there is simply less language from these children than from their hypothetical counterparts.

We know that children learn more in their first year than they will ever again learn, and that by the time they are five they will gain, not only knowledge—about half of a lifetime's worth—but the patterns and styles of learning that will shape their lives. Every moment of their young lives is a learning experience. How do they learn, these tiny infants?

The First Year

They learn, first, by doing something—accidentally or purposefully; moving, acting in a way that interacts with their own bodies and with things around them, their environment. As a result, something else happens—feedback: a bodily response, or an environmental one. If the results are satisfying or provide the needed (or desired) response, they do it again—a constant process of experimentation, exploration, and repetition and expansion: learning. If the results are unsatisfying, or it nothing happens, then the doing is not repeated, and the impulse and potential learning disappear.

In terms of learning, it does not much matter why the feedback is missing. Whether because their bodies are in some way damaged and cannot provide it (the biological risk factor of the Tjossem definition), or because the environment does not or can not provide it (the environmental risk factor); if it is not there, the child does not learn.

If it is there—because of intact, normal bodies and supportive, responsive environments—learning seems to happen almost by osmosis; children observe, notice, imitate, respond, repeat, and learn. How do we learn our native language (the "mother tongue" of linguistics)? This feat, which is completely taken for granted, is the most complex task that we will ever accomplish. How did we learn it? We learned it simply by existing in a speaking community; but recognizing that these bits of sound, parts of our surrounding environment, carry meaning, and by associating these coded noises with the fabric of our lives. We learned it by a kind of osmosis; we almost absorbed it, this incredible human ability to speak and to understand the speaking of others.

An important key to the difference between this "normal process" of learning and that of children at risk lies in the fact that these children do not learn by osmosis. They do not automatically absorb what we consider normal societal learning. Whether at biological or environmental risk, they do not receive the subtle signs and stimuli that produce the even, developmental growth of intact, normal children. Developmental processes are interrupted; there are gaps in learning; frequently the feedback signals that they

do get are faulty, because they have not been able to process them accurately from the beginning. And so, as the song says, ". . . they have to be carefully taught."

They have to be taught to explore—to focus on and notice the essential environmental clues that give us language, a context, a society. They must be taught to discover, to notice, to observe. Only then can they utilize the stimulation from inside and outside their bodies that is essential to growth and learning and living in this world.

Successfully Teaching At-Risk Children

The teacher uses structure, routine and familiarity to frame and order the class time. Well-known and well-loved opening and closing songs, with familiar movements and "old shoe" comfort begin and end the session, which lasts as long as the children's tolerance and attention do. Today's session is quite lengthy; tomorrow's may be very brief. Within the frame of the familiar, the teacher provides for the children the exploration options that they cannot yet initiate themselves. She designs the stimulation sources that are absent from their environments, and presents the sources in the focused ways (One thing at a time!) that break through the barriers of sensory loss that their bodies and brains may have suffered. She helps replace the stimulation loss that these children have experienced, through musical input that is auditory, motor, and visual, and through encouraging equally multisensory responses: moving, singing, playing, looking at and manipulating instruments and other objects, and talking.

But putting stimulation into the childrens' lives is only half the story. The other side is that the children's ability to "screen" or monitor sensory input is frequently limited or eliminated by at-risk factors. One of the most obvious and widespread characteristics of at-risk children is their propensity for overstimulation; a risk for the teacher is that stimulus overload will trigger out-of-control responses such as hyperactivity and perseveration (not being able to stop or slow down an activity once it has begun, but continuing it in a more and more driven, compulsive way).

From the literature concerning autistic children comes an interesting corollary to the stimulus/overload dichotomy of the at-risk child. Believed to be a central nervous system communicative disorder, childhood autism is not a single "condition" but a combination of various syndromes producing a continuum of degree and involvement. Autistic children have almost no tolerance for excessive (or even normal) external stimuli. They are extraordinarily hyperirritable: that is, they cannot distinguish between figure and ground, between detail and background. They seem to be extremely distractable; actually, they pay too much attention to everything. The self-stimulative behavior—the *autisms*—so characteristic of these children are in fact devices for shutting out the world and its incessant invasions; autistic children use autisms to turn inward and to ward off the world's assaults. Successful teachers of autistic children begin by literally emptying the child's environment of all stimuli—except the one item (a visual element, an object, or a sound) that the teacher wishes to use as the focus of learning. All the clutter, all the distractions, all the items that pull attention in dozens of directions are gone. "Austere" is hardly the world for the learning space that results, but now the odds are far better that the child's attention can be caught and held.

Of course, the at-risk child is not imprisoned by overstimulation to the extent that the autistic child is, but there is an echo of the same reality. So what about the quality—and quantity—of the musical stimulus? Should one keep the class very low key, use quiet, slow music, not encourage the children to respond lest they respond too much?

Of course not.

Musical Activities

The class I'm watching is doing all kinds of things: singing heartily, often (though not always) songs with a repeated single word or short phrase: "Aaann-iee!" or "Love, love, love, love!" They sing in dialogue too, back and forth across the circle, or in a singing conversation with the teacher. They move—a lot! They point to hearts or dots or chipmunks on a chart. Later, they jump on a floor-sized version of the chart, controlling how fast or slowly the others sing by the rate of their enthusiastic jumping. They listen to many kinds of music: instrumental, sung, or plucked from a synthesizer (sounds which they imitate earnestly with body shapes and body sounds). The music is energetic and rhythmic and gentle and funny and a little somber, sometimes: their responses run the same gamut. So why aren't the children getting oversaturated with stimulation—climbing the walls and screaming and acting out?

Because the teacher has carefully structured all this input, this stimulation, in two ways: She has limited the stimulation to one thing at a time and only one: one stimulus, one response; and she has presented the material in such a way that each child, at any moment, has only one point of focus. He or she thinks about one thing at a time, does one thing at a time, listens for one thing at a time. Each step comes straight out of the previous one, transferring to the next; and each task has been partly prepared for the child by the task that came before.

I watch, surprised, as twelve children take turns jumping from heart to heart on a chart on the floor; the hearts represent the tones of a brief melody charted on the floor. All the children can do it—remarkable in itself—and each does it in his or her own way. The others watch with great interest and sing the melody each time a child "performs" it. They are attentive and interested. It is great fun to watch each one put an individual stamp on the activity and make it his or her own.

And what marvelous learning is going on—out of the musical experience, without which nothing would be happening, radiating into the kinds of learning that these children need so very much:

1. *Social skills:* taking turns, and following instructions, and waiting!

2. *Temporal skills:* starting and stopping and finding a basic pulse, a steady beat, and then altering it (changing tempo) without losing its evenness and ongoingness.

3. *Spatial skills:* finding directions (up and down) aurally, from the music, then relating them to vertical space (touching the hearts on the chart), and translating them to horizontal space (the floor). This is a difficult maneuver for anyone with the kinds of neurological difficulties for which these children are at risk.

4. *Skills* that will be needed for *academic growth:* Understanding that the hearts and dots stand for (represent; "are") the tones of the melody or the sounds of the even pulse.

Within the musical context, accompanied by the joy of making and sharing music, is another "environment"—one that provides all the essential properties for expediting learning.

Music and the Development of Language

There is still another difference between these children and their more intact counterparts, that of language development. Many of the components of both biological and environmental at-risk factors suggest interference with normal acquisition of speech. Real parallels exist between language and music. Music and language share all of their respective basic concepts: both exist in time, and are linear in their formal organization; both comprise pitch, duration, and timbre with all the accompanying attributes. Hence, experience with music, which tends to be more accessible to children who have trouble dealing with the meaning load of language, can be a model for experience with language, providing a "safe" arena for learning their common concepts.

While the development of language parallels in many ways the development of music, there are basic differences that underscore the wider versatility of music as an attractive domain for developing language skills. In language and music, speaking or singing functions (expressive activities) are very different from those of listening (receptive activity). Reading and interpreting words or notation (receptive activities) differ in yet other ways. Motor functions involved in vocalizing and playing instruments (expressive activities) demonstrate still different aspects. But music, free of the meaning load of a true language, allows a wide range of mode, preference, and response activity in any or all of these differing functions, whatever the maturity level of the child, or the choice of musical learning setting (individual participation, large group experience, and so on).

Some years ago, Howard Gardner discussed the symbol-using skills of normal children and brain-damaged adults, with attention to the disparity of the seemingly similar skills discussed above. He suggested that

> musical capacities may be organized [in the brain] in idiosyncratic ways across individuals. Perhaps most individuals learn in rather similar ways to speak. . ., but the organization of music in the brain may differ dramatically depending on whether one has learned an instrument, what instrument one favors, whether one plays by ear, the extent to which one sings, and so on.[4]

Thus, music seems to afford us a variety of ways to help children learn and practice language-like concepts and skills; its accessibility for young children seems limited only by its presence in the children's environments. (Obviously these learnings can't take place if the children have no music!) Experience with music, which is much more accessible to children who have trouble accessing the meaning load of language, can model language experiences, providing another arena for learning their common concepts.

The relationship between language and music can extend into the structuring of learning experience in both areas. A common model for language learning is the expanded play experience model; the clinician begins with an experiential statement, then encourages the child to change just one thing at a time: "I catch the ball." What else can we do with the ball? (Throw it; roll it.) What else can we catch? (A fish; a firefly.) Each change expands the experience—and the language comprehension. The music teacher begins with a little tune, a melody moving upward. What else can we do with this music? (Move down instead of up; make it slower, faster; play it over and over again; make it very loud.) What else can we do with this rattle? (Shake it hard; play it on my hand; make it very quiet.) Each change expands the experience, and, with the language and music comprehension, explores the nature of the sound world that is the core of each discipline.

There is yet another aspect of commonality that can serve us as we guide and nurture these children—that of style and preference. Recent research in speech pathology shows us that when children do find words and begin to speak, from the very beginning they have definite preferences as to how to go about it. There are two basic styles into which children's speech preferences fall. Some start right out naming things, labeling objects, using single words to differentiate and identify; they are interested in objects, the things in their world. They are already "referential speakers," and their language will continue to develop in this direction. Other children begin speaking by using short phrases which are interactive, and which usually have social implications: "Hi, baby!" "Go bye bye!" "Want doll!"

These children probably are and will be "expressive speakers" whose style already involves interaction with people.

Neither of these styles is "better"; both are effective forms of language in the child's world, as they will be in the adult world. But we should encourage these young speakers, while respecting and celebrating their preferences and their differences, to develop "the other" style as well, to increase their effectiveness in communication and expand their options. Music, too, offers infinite opportunity for choices and preferences. None of the choices or preferences are "better," but the more experiences children have with all kinds of music and musical responses, the more they may be able to develop "the other" styles: tolerating differences, relishing novelty, and continuing to expand their developing curiosity about the world.

At a recent colloquium where music educators, teachers of young children, and speech pathologists shared experiences, a special music educator commented:

> Recent research in the "whole language movement" seems to indicate that the more natural the activities and the more "holistic" the introduction to the material, the more the child is able to assimilate and learn the material. Activities in the arts, specifically music, [provide] a natural way for children to encounter language in a relaxed and enjoyable manner. One of the strengths of music... is that its non-verbal [aspects] may provide communicative and developmentally appropriate activities which enhance not only musical development, but language development through use of different avenues of auditory comprehension and expressive communication. [5]

The children have sung their "goodbye" song, and a few have come over and said goodbye to me. Teachers and children are gathering and moving on, and they begin to hurry or drift from the room. Somehow I feel that something has changed, has happened during these past moments.

Perhaps we have come full circle. In company with our three- and four- year-old children at risk, and in the arena of musical experiences, we may have found ways to teach exploration, to structure for expanded experiences and widened horizons for learning, and to plant the seeds of curiosity to keep those horizons open through a lifetime.

Notes

1. L. Rosetti, *High Risk Infants: Indentification, Assessment, and Intervention* (Boston: Little, Brown and Company, 1989).

2. T. Tjossem, "Children At Risk for Development Delay," in *Early Intervention for Handicapped and At-Risk Infants* (Denver: Love Publishing, 1987).

3. S. Sparks, et al., *Infants at Risk for Communication Disorders* (Kalamazoo, MI: Western Michigan University Department of Speech Pathology and Audiology, n.d.).

4. H. Gardner, "Brain Damage: A Window on the Mind," *Saturday Review* (9 Aug. 1975).

5. E. D. Bernstorf, transcribed from "Language Intervention in Infants and Toddlers," Department of Communicative Disorders, The Wichita State University, 23 Nov. 1990.

Betty Welsbacher is professor of music education at The Wichita State University in Wichita, Kansas, where she developed and teaches in the special music education degree emphasis program.

Planning appropriate musical experiences for children under the age of five years requires knowledge of their skill levels and development. Evaluation of young children is the only means to access this knowledge. Linda Miller Walker maintains that the practice of "extending downward"—using procedures and materials intended for elementary grade children to evaluate younger children is obsolete and inappropriate. An overview of related theoretical principles is included as a basis for evaluations that "fit" young children. Existing music assessments are explored for their appropriateness, along with recommendations for use. The article concludes with a discussion of observation procedures and considerations for teachers and researchers.

Assessment in Early Childhood Music

❖

BY LINDA MILLER WALKER

hat is assessment? When applied to young children, assessment can mean different things to different people. Most music educators would agree that assessment is an ongoing process of collecting data for purposes of evaluation. As used in this chapter, evaluation refers to the overall process of making judgments about a child's musical behaviors or development. Everything that we do to determine a young child's musical behaviors and development is considered evaluative and involves assessment. Thus, evaluation and assessment are processes in determining the musical learnings of prekindergarten children.

A variety of tests are designed to measure musical aptitude and ability, musical achievement, musical performance, as well as attitudes and other affective behaviors. Assessment of young children may involve either of the above. Regardless of what is being assessed, the test used must be valid and reliable. Radocy and Boyle state that "music test content and design must reflect the test's intended function" and "consideration for the general developmental level, academic level, and test-taking experience of the test takers."[1] The type of instrument used may be formal or informal, standardized or nonstandardized and may take place in a structured or nonstructured environment.

Why Assess?

The purpose of assessment in early childhood music is to determine what skills a child has mastered and what skills are not yet mastered. Knowledge of the child's skill levels dictates what specific instructional programs should be offered for young children. Musical assessments also assist in the development of music aptitude. It is important that teachers determine next steps in sequencing appropriate musical experiences for preschool children.

The critical period theory offers evidence that children grow and learn more quickly from birth to age five than at any other time in life. Gordon states that "regardless of the level of music aptitude a child is born with, he [she] must have favorable early informal and formal experiences in music in order to maintain that level of potential."[2] The early years of life are significantly important for enhancing musical development, improving intellectual performance, and establishing a base for future learning.[3]

Thus, the goal of assessing the musical behaviors of young children is to obtain objective information necessary to make decisions about educational programs for this age level.

Related Theoretical Principles

Assessment procedures for preschool children have often been adaptations of what was found to be useful with elementary-aged children. The practice of extending materials and procedures downward can be avoided when music educators understand early childhood development and current promising practices in music for young children. Different procedures for assessing this age group need to be established, based on known theoretical principles and developmentally appropriate practices. Piaget's views of child development provide a framework about the nature of children from birth to seven years of age and how they may be evaluated.[4] Although his developmental sequence has been criticized, it continues to be the basis by which other approaches are examined.

In the sensorimotor stage (birth through age two) the object world is primary and information is received through the senses. At this age, children do not differentiate between when an object is present or not present if it is not immediate in the environment or to the senses. Later the infants construct object permanence, and understand that objects continue to exist outside of their own experience. Assessment procedures that are geared toward physical manipulation of musical materials in the environment are preferred.

The preoperational stage-child (age two to seven) has not yet developed mental structures needed for logical or abstract thought. Judgment during this period is based on reasoning from particular to particular without a logical connection. Parents and teachers can get clues about children's levels of cognitive development by observing their spontaneous questions and responses to questions, preferences for materials or kinds of play, use of language, and occasionally, the sort of humor a child shows. Research indicates that Piaget's conservation tasks offer a direct way of assessing levels of cognitive development.[5] To meet the developmental needs of prekindergarten children, however, assessment procedures should rely heavily on structural observations of their natural music-making behaviors in a nonthreatening environment. A valid instrument should result in "thick" descriptive data.

What has been done in music settings that fits the developmental needs of young children? The Pillsbury Foundation School was set up to study the music of children ages two to six. Musical behaviors were observed, recorded, and described. Psychological, social, and activity factors were considered important and analyzed. The Pillsbury faculty believed that children's musical learnings were inseparable from other learnings because they all took place simultaneously. Freedom for the children to explore their own interests, make sounds appropriate to them, and to pursue their own purposes was crucial. Children were free to explore a wide variety of musical instruments, create spontaneous chants and songs, to move, and to experiment with musical notation.[6] Young children need to be allowed freedom to explore within music learning centers before being subjected to rigid test procedures.

Fewell described three major theoretical viewpoints about assessing young children.[7] Within the developmental theory, a child's cognitive, fine and gross motor, language, and social behavior skills are evaluated either through attainment or lack thereof. These data are then compared with peers in a norm group. Behavioral theory follows a sequence wherein behaviors are observed, objectives define what behaviors should be developing, performance criteria are determined to define new behaviors, and progress is measured systematically. Data are then compared with the predetermined criteria. Adaptive-transactive theory emphasizes interactions or transactions between a child and external stimuli (social or environmental).

Additional research in child development indicates that young children learn best when playing, when they are actively involved in music, and when a multisensory approach to learning is used.[8] However, given the theoretical bases from which to assess young children, the evaluations often look and are different. Evaluations work best if they fit the tasks by which very young children learn music. If the task is aural or kinesthetic, then the evaluation should be aural or kinesthetic. We can begin by using formal or informal observation procedures. Only when children are developmentally ready should the teacher/researcher evaluate using procedures such as paper-and-pencil tests.

Music Assessments

Several music evaluation instruments are available for use with young children. Scores of prekindergarten children on some of the tests are low, indicating that test procedures and items for this age level are not very reliable. Three instruments designed for young children are selected for examination: Primary Measures of Music Audiation (PMMA), Simons Measurements of Music Listening Skills (SMMLS), and the Motoric Music Skills Test (MMST).

The Primary Measures of Music Audiation, designed for children in kindergarten through grade three, include tonal and rhythm patterns in both major and minor tonalities.[9] The forty-item test is standardized, yields an objective tonal subtest score, rhythm subtest score, and a composite score. The author states that "because the PMMA includes only the two basic constructional dimensions of music aptitude, it is short and simple enough to be administered with sufficient validity to very young children." Admin-

istration time is twenty minutes for each test and the tonal test must be administered first. Children are required to identify same/different sounds heard on a tape recording by drawing a circle around specified same/different pictures.

Percentile norms for each grade measure basic aptitude at the child's own developmental level. To assist with the development of music aptitude, teachers and parents should supplement PMMA scores with other available information about the child. The PMMA manual includes applications of test results to teach music most effectively. For kindergarten, the composite split-halves reliability is .90, test-retest reliability is .74. Since the tests are not designed for children below kindergarten, no reliability or validity is established for preschool.

The Simons Measurements of Music Listening Skills is a criterion-referenced test designed for children also in grades K–3.[10] Nine subtests measure the abilities of children to aurally recognize the direction of a melodic movement, melodic movement as stepping or leaping, a musical sound consisting of one or more tones, chord changes, meter in two or three, same or different tonal patterns, same or different rhythm patterns, soft or loud dynamic levels, and fast or slow tempos. Administration time for each subtest is five to eight minutes. The entire test, including verbal instruction, demonstration items, practice items, and test items is tape recorded to assure consistent administration. Children are not required to read or write, but must respond to aural items by marking pictures or large numbers. Subtests may be used individually.

The SMMLS manual supplies scoring procedures, interpretation of results as well as mean scores and standard deviations for 315 public school children in grades K–3. Low kindergarten scores indicate that the test is unsuitable for this age. Measures of validity and reliability are unavailable. No scores are available for prekindergarten.

The Motoric Music Skills Test includes forty-four items measuring motor music skills through five subtests: motor pattern coordination, eye-hand coordination, speed of movement, range of movement, and compound factors.[11] The test was designed and piloted with 808 public school children ages three through six. Administration time is fifteen to twenty minutes.

Children are required to use the dominant hand, non-dominant hand, both hands simultaneously as well as both the dominant and non-dominant hands alternately to strike percussion instruments. Additionally, they must strike anyplace and in a designated place on the playing surface. Validity (content, concurrent, predictive) and reliability (internal consistency, test-retest, interjudge) are established for the instrument. The author states that the instrument "constitutes a sound, reliable, and appropriate measure to assess selected motoric music skills in young children."[12]

Of the three tests (tonal and rhythm aptitude, listening skills, motor skills) only the motor skills test was designed for children younger than five. It also allows children to manipulate objects in the physical environment. By design, the other two tests are not recommended for use with prekindergarten children. They are paper-and-pencil types not effectively used with children below the age of five.

Additional instruments developed for use with young children are designed to measure musical growth, to measure the rhythmic ability of four-year-old children and the effects of rhythmic training, and to examine children's ability to discriminate instrumental timbres.[13] An array of tests have been developed in the writing of doctoral dissertations in music education.

In recent years there has been a wedding of music education research with that in early childhood education and child development. Music educators recognize that knowledge of how children develop generally is invaluable and inseparable from their musical development. Several nonmusical instruments are available. For example, the Bracken Basic Concept Scale includes letter identification, counting, direction, and time sequence.[14] A test developed by Goldman, Fristoe, and Woodcock evaluates children's abilities to discriminate speech sounds through responses to tape-recorded stimuli.[15] The Home Observation for Measurement of the Environment, an assessment of language stimulation, physical environment, and stimulation of academic behavior, is useful in screening all children to identify those "at risk" for school failure.[16]

Contemporary Approaches

Systematic observation techniques allow the teacher/researcher to gather information about young children's specific musical behaviors, other academic skills, social skills, and self-help skills. The first step in designing a systematic observation is to decide what behavior will be observed. The specific behavior should be described in observable and measurable terms. Second, how to measure the behavior needs to be determined. A researcher may use event sampling or duration recording. In event sampling, the observer records the number of times a desired behavior occurs. In duration recording, the observer records when a desired behavior begins and ends. Next, the researcher should decide how often to measure the behavior. The final step in observational procedures is a decision about the method of data collection.

There are three kinds of observational data: narrative, checklist, and rating scales. Narrative data includes anecdotal records, field notes, and descriptions of the setting and conditions for assessment, called ecological or environmental. With narrative data, the recorder describes observed behaviors rather than interprets them. Interpretation is done later in the research process. Structured or unstructured interviews, discussions, and oral reports are also types of narrative data.

Checklist data are limited to specific behaviors and situations that are not open to debate, such as age, race, and sex of the subject. The checklist is structured and highly objective. Behaviors to be observed are selected and designed in advance of the observation. The researcher classifies behaviors, into predetermined categories, by frequency or duration. Judgment is qualitative and no quantification is completed until after data collection.

The most widely used type of observational data is the rating scale. The rating scale involves judgment about what a particular behavior means. When using the rating scale an observer has to make interpretations of the data. Ratings are classified as numerical, graphic, standard, cumulated points, and forced-choice. According to Medley and Mitzel, ratings suffer drawbacks due to rater biases and lack of agreement between raters.[17]

Some Considerations

Has the music education profession found or perfected the most effective means of assessment for young "at risk" children? Prekindergarten children? Do we need to combine research efforts by developing an evaluation instrument to examine specific musical responses—to be used by all researchers interested in a particular area? Are we reinventing, but not perfecting, the wheel with each dissertation?

Assessment of the musical behaviors of young children need not be just a determination of their ability to match pitch or respond perfectly on rhythmic tasks. Music educators need to examine musical responses in relation to the whole child, ask new or different questions, and nuture developing musicality. We need to consider the source of the information that we are trying to gain. That source is the prekindergarten child who is different from us developmentally. For those of us who can, try and remember what is was like to be a little person.

The research literature is replete with considerations for assessing young children.[18] Regard-less of what musical behaviors we assess or how we assess them, the development of young children should be considered. Young children are:

- unable to attend for a long period of time;
- easy to tire and will not tolerate long, structured activities;
- easily distracted by interesting or new things or a change in routine;
- egocentric and have not developed social awareness to want to do the best job;
- often fearful of strangers or strange environments and situations, and may not perform well in certain situations due to shyness, anxiety, or separation from significant others; and
- sometimes uncooperative and will assert independence by noncompliance to commands or instructions, especially from strangers.

Some suggestions for teachers/researchers include:

- avoid testing in one day because the behaviors of young children vary from day to day and situation to situation;
- make certain that test instruments are appropriate for the age level and skill level of the child;
- be sure that the logistics for testing and the tasks fit the child's age and previous learnings;
- establish some type of rapport with the child;
- if necessary, invite parents to be present with infants;
- scrutinize parent reports carefully as they may overestimate or underestimate the child's abilities;
- use natural environments for assessment as they are most likely to increase responsiveness of the child;
- avoid drawing conclusions on bits and pieces of information, which may result in inaccurate views of the child's strength, weaknesses, and developmental abilities.

Summary

There is still much to be known about what preschool children do with music and what music does to them. Increased knowledge is needed in order to design the best instructional programs for this age group. Only through using the most appropriate assessment procedures, based on sound reasoning and developmental levels, can we begin to meet the musical needs at this critical age.

Research in early childhood music is still developing and the future looks good. Developmental, behavioral, and adaptive-transactive theories provide one base for current and future research endeavors. The fields of early childhood education and child development are springboards to a richer assessment of young children's musical behaviors. Both music and nonmusic assessments are already in place as guidelines, albeit observational assessment procedures appear to be the most effective for use in early childhood. Consideration of the Music Educators National Conference position statement about what is a developmentally appropriate program of singing, moving, listening, creating, playing instruments, and responding to visual and verbal representations of sound is a must.

Notes

1. R. Radocy and J. Boyle, *Measurement and Evaluation of Musical Experiences* (New York: Schirmer, 1987), 103–04.

2. E. Gordon, *The Nature, Description, Measurement, and Evaluation of Music Aptitudes* (Chicago: G.I.A. Publications, 1987), 8.

3. B. Andress, "Music for Every Stage," *Music Educators Journal* 76 (October 1989): 22–27; P. Michel, "The Optimum Development of Music Abilities in the First Years of Life," *Psychology of Music* 1 (1973): 14–20; J. Feierabend, "Music in Early Childhood," *Design for Arts in Education* 91 (1990): 15–20; J. Hunt, "The Psychological Basis for Using Preschool Enrichment as an Antidote for Cultural Deprivation," *Merrill-Palmer Quarterly* 10 (1964): 209–48; C. Scott, "How Children Grow—Musically," *Music Educators Journal* 76, (October 1989): 28–31; R. Hess and D. Croft, *Teachers of Young Children*, 2d ed. (Boston: Houghton Mifflin, 1975); and S. Kenney, "Music Centers: Freedom to Explore," *Music Educators Journal* 76 (October 1989): 32–36.

4. J. Piaget, *The Child's Conception of the World* (London: Routledge & Kegan Paul, 1951); and J. Piaget, *The Judgment and Reasoning of the Child* (London: Routledge & Kegan Paul, 1951).

5. D. Elkind, *Child Development and Education* (New York: Oxford University Press, 1976); and M. Pflederer, "The Responses of Children to Musical Tasks Embodying Piaget's Principal of Conservation," *Journal of Research in Music Education* 12, no.4 (1964): 251–68.

6. G. Moorhead and D. Pond, *Music of Young Children* (Santa Barbara, CA: Pillsbury Foundation Studies, 1978).

7. R. Fewell, "The Team Approach to Infant Education," in *Educating Handicapped Infants: Issues in Development and Intervention*, ed. S. Garwood and R. Fewell (Rockville, MD: Aspen Systems, 1983).

8. M. Brand and D. Fernie, "Music in the Early Childhood Curriculum," *Young Children* 37 (1983): 321–26; L. Miller, "A Description of Children's Musical Behaviors: Naturalistic," *Bulletin of the Council for Research in Music Education* 87 (1986): 1–16; and M. Zimmerman, *Musical Characteristics of Children* (Reston, VA: Music Educators National Conference, 1971).

9. E. Gordon, *Primary Measures of Music Audiation* (Chicago: G.I.A. Publications, 1979).

10. G. Simons, *Simons Measurements of Music Listening Skills* (Chicago: Stoelting, 1976).

11. J. Gilbert, "Assessment of Motoric Music Skill Development in Young Children: Test Con-

struction and Evaluation Procedures," *Psychology of Music* 7 (1979): 3–12.

12. Gilbert, *"Assessment of Motoric Music Skill Development,"* 10.

13. M. Greenberg, *Preschool Music Achievement Test* (Honolulu: Center for Research in Early Childhood Education, 1970); R. McDowell, "The Development and Implementation of a Rhythmic Ability Test Designed for Four-Year-Old Preschool Children," Doctoral Dissertation, University of North Carolina, *Dissertation Abstracts International* 35 (1974): 2029A; and D. Loucks, "The Development of an Instrument to Measure Instrumental Timbre Concepts of Four-Year-Old Children: A Feasibility Study," Doctoral Dissertation, Ohio State University, *Dissertation Abstracts International* 35 (1974): 5448A.

14. B. Bracken, *Bracken Basic Concept Scale* (Columbus, OH: Charles E. Merrill, 1984).

15. R. Goldman, M. Fristoe, and R. Woodcock, *Goldman-Fristoe-Woodcock Test of Auditory Discrimination* (Circle Pines, NM: American Guidance Service, 1974).

16. R. Bradley and B. Caldwell, "The HOME Inventory: A Validation of the Preschool Scale for Black Children," *Child Development* 52 (1981): 708–10.

17. D. Medley and H. Mitzel, "Measuring Classroom Behavior by Systematic Observation," in *Handbook of Research on Teaching,* ed. N. Gage (Chicago: Rand McNally, 1963).

18. C. Dunst and R. Rheingrover, "Discontinuity and Instability in Early Development: Implications for Assessment," *Topics in Early Childhood Special Education* 1 (1981): 49–60; I. Evans and R. Nelson, "Assessment of Child Behavior Problems," in *Handbook of Behavioral Assessment,* ed. A. Ciminero, K. Calhoun, and H. Adams (New York: John Wiley & Sons, 1977); R. MacTurk and J. Neisworth, "Norm-Referenced and Criterion Based Measures with Preschoolers," *Exceptional Children* 45, (1978): 34–39; and A. Mendelson and R. Atlas, "Early Childhood Assessment: Paper and Pencil for Whom?" *Readings in Early Childhood Education* (1977): 269–71.

Linda Miller Walker is assistant professor of music education at Kent State University, where she teaches undergraduate and graduate courses and coordinates K–4 music in the Demonstration School program.